ACTS 1-12
BIRTH
OF THE BODY

RAY STEDMAN

**VISION HOUSE
PUBLISHERS**

Santa Ana, California 92705

BIRTH OF THE BODY

Copyright © 1974 by Vision House Publishers, Santa Ana, California 92705

Library of Congress Catalog Number 74-82549
ISBN-088449-013-0 (paperback)
ISBN-088449-019-X (cloth)

Printed in the United States of America.

DEDICATION

To the elders of
Peninsula Bible Church,
faithful colaborers in Christ.

"You shall receive a crown of glory."

Contents

Chapter 1 Out of the Shadows   11
A Building and a Body ... Dressed in Flesh ... By Convincing Proofs ... The Blessing of Abraham ... Pictures of the Spirit ... Quiet Power ... Eyes on the Lord ... An Assured Return ... The Final Link

Chapter 2 The Birthday   25
A Foundation of Twelve ... The Last Payment ... The Lord's Decision ... The Task of the Twelve ... Two Loaves into One ... Members of One Another ... Purifying Passion

Chapter 3 Beyond Tongues   37
No Interpreters Needed ... Curiosity and Ridicule ... Explaining Reality ... In the Last Days ... Is It the Same Gift? ... The Need for Warning

Chapter 4 Confrontation   47
The Standard Man ... Putting Evil to Death ... Not One Challenge ... Pointing Toward Jesus ... Evidence of Lordship

Chapter 5 The Essential Ingredients   55
Change Your Mind ... A New Beginning ... God's

6

Choice, Our Choice . . . To Experience Life . . . Forgiving One Another . . . Fear and Favor

Chapter 6 The Healing Hand of Jesus   62
Why Look? . . . No Magic . . . The Ground for Witness . . . Signs of an Apostle . . . Inner Miracles

Chapter 7 The Only Solution   70
Begin with the Facts . . . The Forces of Guilt . . . Out of Ignorance . . . Refreshment and Restoration . . . The Personal Question

Chapter 8 The Threat of the Resurrection   78
Cause for Alarm . . . Death is Death . . . Send up the Cornerstone! . . . Truth with Power

Chapter 9 When Obedience is Wrong   86
An Illegal Act . . . Whom to Obey? . . . Everything's Under Control . . . To Carry Out His Plan . . . Shakedown

Chapter 10 Great Power, Great Grace, Great Fear   95
Belonging to Each Other . . . Making Life Visible . . . The Law of Love . . . Son-of-a-Gift . . . Cutting off the Life

Chapter 11 Times of Peril   104
Striking Powers . . . What Greater Works? . . . Not Bound . . . Behind the Opposition . . . Worthy to Suffer

Chapter 12 Seven Choice Men   112
Attack from Within . . . According to the Gift . . . Specifications . . . Sharing the Ministry . . . Evidence of Life

Chapter 13 The Issue is Jesus   120
Charge and Countercharge . . . Pointed Contrasts . . . Failure and Faith . . . The Two-Edged Sword . . . Faithful Unto Death

Chapter 14 God Has the Edge 131
The Real Thing... Counterfeit Christianity... The Devil Joins the Church... Into One Body... No Repentance

Chapter 15 Have Spirit, Will Travel 141
Freedom to Interfere... The Man and the Moment... Beginning with This Scripture... Caught up in Joy

Chapter 16 Beloved Enemy 148
Beyond the Border... Exposure and Development... Strength from the Body... Gentiles First ... Filled and Enlightened

Chapter 17 The Yoke of Christ 156
Because He Is Lord... Into the Desert... Paul's Plan... His Greatest Moment... Get Out of Town!

Chapter 18 Three Faces of Death 165
Interrupted Service... Cornelius and the Angel... The Death of Prejudice... Choice, Not Exclusion... Setting Aside All Malice

Chapter 19 Peter and Cornelius 174
Prepared for the Gospel... Man As God Intended... Every Man Must Choose... Holy Interruption... An End to the Matter

Chapter 20 Recognition of a Church 183
Gentle Investigator... Expecting God to Work... To a Young Church... Don't Look Down... Plenty Meets Need

Chapter 21 Let Us Pray 191
No Automatic Deliverance... Seeing Is Not Believing... Called to Participate... Releasing God's Mercy... In Mysterious Ways

Author's Preface

Dr. E.M. Blaiklock, longtime Professor of Classics at the University of New Zealand, has said, "Of all the centuries, the twentieth is most like the first." Despite the obvious technological differences (which are certainly superficial), the truth of Dr. Blaiklock's statement can be demonstrated in several ways, including the position of the church in the world today. Twentieth-century Christians confront a thoroughly secularized and pagan world, just as the first-century Christians did. Persecution of Christians in the twentieth century is far more widespread and at least as violent as it ever was in the first century. The seeds of restless discontent have been widely sown among the nations in our day, and people everywhere are crying out for relief from the sense of emptiness and despair which a widespread materialism has produced.

The major difference between the two centuries is that the virile, growing church of today must contend not only with a secularized society, but also with a secularized church—a vast and torpid body which moves only slowly toward restored vitality. Nevertheless, vitality is returning! In spontaneous upthrusts which are breaking out in many places, the Holy Spirit is restoring the church to the original pattern given in the Scriptures, thereby reviving its pristine power and impact. The changes that have taken place in the church worldwide during the past ten years is phenomenal. The recent Congress for World Evangelization held in Lausanne, Switzerland, reflected many of these changes.

At a time like this nothing could be more helpful to the church than to review again the record of the early church's rise and growth. The same principles which produced explosive growth then will do so today. The same pattern of leadership which prevailed then must prevail again in the twentieth century. The same remarkable power which accounted for the church's success then can and must be found today, for Christ's promise has never changed: "I will build my church, and the gates of hell shall not prevail against it."

These studies on the first twelve chapters of the Book of Acts have been sent forth with the explicit intention of showing how the church of Acts is designed to be normative Christianity. Certain signs and symbols which were present in Acts (and have been made far too much of today) are not as present in the twentieth-century church to the same degree. But that is as it should be, for the roof of a building does not duplicate exactly the foundation, though it is part of the same building and may use much of the same material. While the Great Architect has proceeded with the construction of His building exactly according to the blueprints which He made available at the beginning, a great many well-meaning friends have sought to help the project by building rooms and lean-tos of their own, all made with shoddy, junk materials. Ultimately these side structures will all be torn down as so much scaffolding, and the true building will be revealed just as the Architect planned it.

Through the dust and haze of construction it may help to see the emerging building more clearly if we study the blueprints carefully. To this end these studies are presented. They were originally part of a series of messages on the Book of Acts which were preached to the attentive congregation of the Peninsula Bible Church in Palo Alto, California. I am indebted particularly to Mrs. Jean McAllister for their present re-edited form, and to Mr. Paul Winslow for his untiring efforts in bringing them to publication.

Chapter One

Out of the Shadows

Acts 1:1-14

The Book of Acts unveils one of the most exciting dramas of the Bible. Though the full name of the Book is *The Acts of the Apostles*, only Peter, James, John, and Paul appear prominently as apostles. Through the centuries, Christians have shortened this title to simply *The Acts*. This is an appropriate name, for Acts is truly a book of action, showing God at work through the living body of Christ, the church.

One of the nicer things said about today's nominal church is that it is irrelevant. Many people look upon the church as nothing but a collection of colorless religious creeps who come to church to sit with blank stares on their faces. This lifelessness of today's church may well have stimulated the famous remark by Nietzsche, the pagan philosopher: "If you want me to believe in your Redeemer, you'll have to look a lot more redeemed!"

Some people think of the church as a group of religious bureaucrats who are forever issuing pronouncements to which no one pays any attention. Others think of it as a group of plastic hypocrites trying to play waterboy to the game of life; whenever real issues need to be faced, the church stands off to one side and says "Me too." Some people view the church as a group of "good time Charlies" who never entertain a serious thought, never think deeply about life, and never care enough about other people to bother getting their hands dirty.

In all honesty we must admit that there is much justification for these charges. But they are true only because the church so easily forgets what it really is. When it operates the way it was intended to, the church is the most important body of people of any era—far above and beyond any other human entity. The church is actually the secret government of earth. As Paul the Apostle says, it is "the pillar and bulwark of the truth" (1 Tim. 3:15), that is, the source and support of all realistic knowledge of life. This is what the church is supposed to be in its day-to-day life on earth.

A Building and a Body

In our study of the Book of Acts we are privileged eye-witnesses of the birth and growth of this amazing phenomenon, which is still present in the twentieth century. In Paul's Letter to the Ephesians he employs two symbols for the church—two major figures that help us to understand what the church is really like. At the end of the first chapter Paul says that the church is a body. He speaks of "his [Christ's] body, the fulness of him who fills all in all" (Eph. 1:23). So the church is a living organism; it is part of the life of Jesus Christ present on this earth. At the close of the second chapter the Apostle says the church is like a building, "members of the household of God, built upon the foundation of the apostles and prophets," which grows into a holy temple designed by the Spirit for the habitation of God (Eph. 2:19-22). So in one sense the church is like a building and in another it is like a body. Yet certain things are common to both these ideas. For one thing, both a building and a body are inhabited by a person. The central thing about the church, therefore, is its relationship to a Person. This personal relationship is what we shall see developing in the Book of Acts.

There is intense conflict throughout the Book, but the conflict is met by ringing confidence. Acts is a record of power in the midst of persecution, of life and health pouring from a living Christ into a sick society through the channel of obscure men and women very much like you and me. The Book of Acts fills the gap between the Gospels and the Book of Romans, making it possible for us to fully understand the New Testament. At the end of the Gospels we find a handful of Jews gathered in Jerusalem talking about a kingdom that is to come to Israel. In the Book of Romans we find an apostle who is not even mentioned in the Gospels and who was not even one of the twelve; he writes to a band of Christians in the capital city of Rome, talking about his plans to travel to the ends of the earth. The Book of Acts tells us how this happened and why this change occurred.

The key to the Book is found in the introduction, where the essential strategy by which Jesus Christ proposes to change the world is revealed—a strategy which is the secret of the revolutionary character of the church when it is operating as it was intended to operate. This strategy is given to us in the first two verses of Acts:

> In the first book, O Theophilus, I have dealt with all that Jesus began to do and teach, until the day when he was taken up, after he had given commandment through the Holy Spirit to the apostles whom he had chosen (Acts 1:1,2).

The writer here is Dr. Luke, that beloved physician who accompanied Paul on his journeys. We do not know how Luke became a Christian, though it was probably through the ministry of the Apostle Paul. Luke was Paul's companion through danger, hardship, trial, and endless difficulty up and down the length and breadth of the Roman Empire. He wrote two books of the New Testament—the Gospel According to Luke and the Book of Acts. Acts is written to a young man named Theophilus, and that is all we know about him. His name indicates that Theophilus was probably a young Greek, perhaps a new convert to Christianity whom Luke met somewhere and to whom he is explaining what Christianity is all about.

It may seem strange that Theophilus is not mentioned anywhere else in Scripture, but anyone with a name like Theophilus might well tend to remain hidden most of the time! I had a friend whose middle initial was "T", and once at a party a friend of his announced that he had discovered what the "T" stood for: Theophilus, because when the doctor first saw this baby he said, "That's the awful-est baby I ever saw!" The name actually means "loved of God," indicating that this young man was probably a Christian. We are indebted to Theophilus for sharing his letters with us, for otherwise we would not have the Gospel of Luke or the Book of Acts.

Dressed in Flesh

In his first statement Luke says, "In the first book I have dealt with all that Jesus *began* to do and teach. . . ." The Gospel of John says, " The Word became flesh and dwelt among us" (John 1:14). Jesus as a man came to begin something—"to do and to teach"— and the record of that beginning is in the Gospels. But Luke clearly implies that this second Book is the continuation of what Jesus began to do. In a very real sense Acts is not the acts of Christians but the continuing acts of Jesus. It is an account of what Jesus continues to do and to teach. In the Gospels He did it in His own physical body, but in the Book of Acts he is doing it through the bodies of men and women who are indwelt by His life. Whether in the Gospels or in Acts, incarnation is the secret strategy by which God changes the world.

Whenever God wants to get a message across to men He does not merely send someone to announce it; his final way of driving it home is to dress the message in flesh and blood. God takes a life and aims it in a certain direction, and then by the manifestation of His own life through the blood and flesh of a human being He makes clear what He has to say. That is the strategy of the Book of Acts. It is the record of incarnation—of men and women possessed by Jesus Christ and manifesting His life every day. Anytime you find a Christianity that is not doing this, it is a false Christianity. No matter how much the pseudo-Christianity may adapt the garb and language of true Christianity, if it is not the activity of human beings possessed and indwelt by the life of Jesus Christ, it is not authentic Christianity. The life of the indwelling Christ is the true power of the church, as we shall see in the Book of Acts.

For this reason the Book of Acts is an unfinished book, for it is still being written. Acts closes abruptly, with an account of Paul living in a rented house in Rome. It almost sounds as if you could turn the next page and begin another new adventure! The Book of Acts is Volume 1, and we today are writing Volume 20. Ours may well be the last volume in the series. I hope that it is!

In this introduction to Acts we learn the historic basis on which· the strategy of incarnation rests and the elements that make up the continuous program by which it operates. The first of these historic elements is the resurrection of Jesus:

> To them [the apostles] he presented himself alive after his passion by many proofs, appearing to them during forty days and speaking of the kingdom of God. And while staying with them he charged them not to depart from Jerusalem. . .(Acts 1:3, 4).

I have already deliberately stopped here to show how Luke stresses the great and central fact of Christian faith: Jesus is alive. That incomparable fact is what thrusts Christianity ten thousand miles ahead of its nearest competitor in the field of religion. There is nothing else like it. Jesus is alive, risen from the dead!

A certain man today who calls himself the Messiah has been announcing that he is the fulfillment of the predictions of the return of the Messiah to earth. He is causing quite a stir among people who are easily influenced by this type of fraud. Whenever I hear of someone like this, my first question is, "Has he risen from the dead?" I'm not interested in any Messiah who hasn't risen from the dead!

By Convincing Proofs

But Jesus Christ has truly risen from the dead: "He presented himself alive after his passion by many (convincing) proofs." The Greek word for "proof" here is a word that includes the idea of being convincing—"infallible," as the King James Version puts it. Luke gives us three categories of proofs that Jesus Christ is alive, though not in as much detail as in other parts of Scripture. These evidences are important, for from the very day of Christ's resurrection certain enemies of Christianity have claimed that the appearances of Jesus were really nothing but hallucinations in the minds of Christ's followers.

"But let me show you," Luke says, "the three categories of proof that he has risen." The first one: he *appeared* to them for a period of forty days. From this word for "appear" we get our word *ophthalmia,* which means literally "the eyeball." In the modern vernacular, these disciples "eyeballed" Jesus for forty days! They saw Him again and again, not merely once, and each time He looked exactly the same. It's hard for a hallucination to accomplish this! Then, too, Christ spoke to them: "*speaking* of the kingdom of God." "We even remember His subject matter," Luke says; "He talked about the kingdom of God." "We saw Him and heard Him—two experiences of our senses that confirmed to us that this was no fantasy, no hallucination." Finally, the ultimate proof was that "He ate with us." (The word "staying" in verse 4 has a marginal reference which gives "eating" as the actual Greek word used.) Those who were with Jesus saw Him eat. They actually saw the food disappear. It must surely be terribly hard to get a hallucination to eat! So Luke says, "This is the proof; He ate with us, so we know He is alive."

This marvelous fact of the resurrection of Jesus is the bedrock upon which all Christian faith ultimately rests. Anytime you are troubled with doubts or are under attack for your faith, come right back to this fundamental fact. The Apostle Paul holds it up for us and says, in effect, to the enemies of Christianity, "Look, if you want to destroy our faith, then disprove this fact. It all rests on this. "If Christ has not been raised, your faith is futile" (1 Cor. 15:17). Throughout the centuries many attempts have been made to disprove the resurrection of Jesus, but none has ever been successful. In fact, in the attempts many skeptics have themselves become convinced by the evidence and have become Christians. The resurrection is fact number one upon which the strategy of incarnation rests.

The second historic fact is referred to here as "the promise of the Father":

And while staying with them he charged them not to depart from Jerusalem, but to wait for the promise of the Father, which, he said, "you heard from me, for John baptized with water, but before many days you shall be baptized with the Holy Spirit." So when they had come together, they asked him, "Lord, will you at this time restore the kingdom to Israel?" He said to them, "It is not for you to know the times or seasons which the Father has fixed by his own authority. But you shall receive power when the Holy Spirit has come upon you; and you shall be my witnesses in Jerusalem and in all Judea and Samaria and to the end of the earth" (Acts 1:4-8).

This passage contains the fourfold characteristic of the baptism of the Holy Spirit. What Jesus said to these eleven disciples (Judas by now having left them) was literally, "Stick around in Jerusalem." That is the Greek expression. "Stick around! Don't go outside the city until the promise of the Father has come upon you." Why? "Because you'll make a mess of it if you try witnessing without this. This is an essential. You can't be an effective Christian if you aren't operating in the power of the Holy Spirit." Every attempt ever made to advance the cause of Christianity which does not arise from this source of power only destroys the message God wants to convey. "Just wait," Jesus says, "for in a few days you will receive the promise of the Father."

The Blessing of Abraham

What did Jesus mean by "the promise of the Father"? First, he indicates that the coming of the Holy Spirit would not be a ritual, but a reality. John, he said, baptized with water. That is a ritual, a shadow, a picture. But the reality will be the actual Spirit Himself coming to live in you. The promise made to Abraham two thousand years ago will be fulfilled in you. God said to Abraham, "I will bless you, and make your name great. . . . And in you all the families of the earth will be blessed" (Gen. 12:2,3 margin). We are not told in Genesis exactly what that blessing is, but in Paul's Letter to the Galatians he tells us very explicitly what the blessing was:

> Christ redeemed us from the curse of the law, having become a curse for us—for it is written, "Cursed be everyone who hangs on a tree"—that in Christ Jesus the blessing of Abraham might come upon the Gentiles, that *we might receive the promise of the Spirit through faith* (Gal. 3:13,14).

There we learn that God promised to give Abraham the Spirit and, through him, to give the blessing (that same Spirit) to everyone who believes, even to the Gentile world. Now does this mean that no one ever received the Holy Spirit until the Day of Pentecost, even though the promise was given to Abraham two thousand years before? Well, no Gentile did, unless he had first become a part of Israel. There is no record of any Gentile believer ever receiving the Holy Spirit until the Day of Pentecost, unless that Gentile first became a Jew.

Pictures of the Spirit

But in the Old Testament there are several accounts of Israelites who were filled with the Spirit. Abraham himself was so filled, because God had promised "I will bless *you*," and that blessing, Paul says, is the promise of the Spirit. But not only Abraham, but also Moses and Joshua and David and many of the kings of Judah were filled with that same Spirit. And certainly all the prophets were Spirit-filled, for Peter tells us that when these prophets predicted the sufferings of Christ and the glory that would follow, they were speaking by means of the Spirit of Christ which was "within them" (1 Pet. 1:11). They were filled with the Holy Spirit and spoke out of that indwelling.

Yet these Old Testament believers came to a realization and experience of the Spirit-filled life only by means of a long, drawn-out process of learning, by means of shadows. They were not given this experience first, as we are, to learn its effects later, but they were taught first by means of pictures, shadows, types, and symbols. The Old Testament is full of these. Aaron's rod that budded, which was kept in the Ark of the Covenant, and the candlestick in the Tabernacle were both pictures of the Holy Spirit illuminating the mind and heart. The widow's cruse of oil which never became empty was a picture of the flowing of the oil of the Spirit in a human life (1 Kgs. 17:8-16). The two olive trees of Zechariah which dripped oil from their branches into the bowls of the golden lampstand are also a picture of the Holy Spirit (Zech. 4:1-14). Ezekiel's river that came pouring out from under the throne of God, growing deeper as it went, is a wonderful picture of the flow and power of the Spirit-filled life (Ezek. 47:1-12). These men of old gradually understood through these symbols what it meant to be filled with the Spirit, and then they experienced this filling by faith.

The last of these symbols or shadows was the baptism of John the Baptist. Jesus said that John was the last of the prophets. We are told of John the Baptist that he was "filled with the Holy Spirit . . . from his mother's womb" (Luke 1:15). He experienced this filling in his own life, but he had to teach it by shadows. As he baptized people in water he thereby taught them that the One who was coming would immediately place them into the body of Christ, making them part of His life. Jesus referred to John the Baptist as the greatest man born of women because he was filled with the Spirit from his mother's womb (Matt. 11:11). But now, Jesus says, there will be no more shadows; now there will be immediate reality. Everyone will *begin* his Christian life on this level.

Jesus had said to these eleven men earlier, "The Spirit of truth . . . dwells *with* you, and he *shall be* in you" (John 14:17). As we have seen, this does not mean that no one in the Old Testament was filled with the Holy Spirit; it only means that these men were *not yet* so filled. Their filling of the Spirit was delayed until it would be available to both Jews and Gentiles. Although they were Jews, they were to be part of a body of both Jews and Gentiles which would be formed by the baptism of the Holy Spirit. Now the Holy Spirit is given to a believer the moment he puts his faith in Jesus. There is no special sign, feeling, or emotional indication of this indwelling. It occurs, as Jesus said it would, when anyone believes in Him. It is the means by which the risen life of Jesus becomes available to us continuously and constantly. All that Jesus is, is made available through all that I am. That is why it is important that the Holy Spirit should come—so that through the Spirit Jesus' life is made available to each of us who trusts in Him.

Quiet Power

Jesus points out that this indwelling is not a *ritual* but *reality*, not a *program* but *power*. The eleven disciples said to Jesus, "Lord, will you at this time restore the kingdom to Israel?" They were thinking in terms of timetables, schedules, and programs. And the church throughout its history has often made this same mistake. But the Lord Jesus said, "That is not for you to know. Times, schedules, and programming are all in the Father's authority. Your task is to be the manifestation of power; the Father will take care of the program. You content yourselves with exercising the power that is given to you, and the Father will put it all together."

Now what kind of power is Jesus talking about? This is a most wonderful thing! It is *resurrection* power. It is the power of a *risen Lord*—there is no way to overthrow it, no way to stop it. Every obstacle thrown in its path is only turned into an opportunity to advance. You can find many demonstrations of this power in the Gospels and in church history. Every attempt to resist the working of the Holy Spirit simply opens the door wider, for this is Christ's resurrection power at work.

It is a glorious kind of power, for it does not need any props or outside help, and it does not borrow anything from the world. It doesn't even need a cup of coffee to get started in the morning! Furthermore, this power works best in a cemetery. It operates most visibly where everything is dull and lifeless. Anyone operating on resurrection power can come in and change the whole scene. Resurrection power changes lives from *within* rather than from without. It does not start on the outside, with the environment, or the circumstances, or the external situation; it starts within and works outward. It does not separate or divide; it harmonizes, heals, draws people together, and breaks down walls of hostility that have been standing sometimes for centuries. It batters these all down and brings people together in harmony. This totally different kind of power is what you receive when you receive the Holy Spirit.

Eyes on the Lord

Jesus also says that this power will result not in *propaganda* but in *witnessing.* Christians are not to be like salesmen going out to peddle a product, nor are they to be recruiters trying to get people to join a religious club. By doing this the church has become false and has lost its power. In contrast, Christ's power has a personal note about it. Jesus says, "You will talk about Me because you will have experienced Me. You will talk about what I have done for you."

The mark of a carnal church is that it loves to talk about itself. These early Christians never witnessed about *the church* at all; they witnessed about *the Lord*—what He could do, how He would work, what a fantastic person He was, how amazing His power was, and what He could do in human hearts. The twentiety-century church too often has its eyes focused on itself. But the early church had its eyes focused on its Lord, and for this reason it was an effective witness for Him.

Finally, this promise of the Father will not be restricted at all, but it will be universal. It will begin in Jerusalem and Samaria and go to the uttermost parts of the earth. It will include all places and all times, and it will make no distinction between classes, races, or sexes.

> In Christ there is no East or West,
> In Him no South or North,

> But one great fellowship of love,
> Throughout the whole wide earth.

An Assured Return

The third historic element which Luke stresses, which runs like a thread throughout the rest of the Book of Acts, is the hope of Christ's return:

> And when he had said this, as they were looking on, he was lifted up, and a cloud took him out of their sight. And while they were gazing into heaven as he went, behold, two men stood by them in white robes, and said, "Men of Galilee, why do you stand looking into heaven? This Jesus, who was taken up from you into heaven, will come in the same way as you saw him go into heaven" (Acts 1:9-11).

What an amazing experience this was! As the disciples were standing on the Mount of Olives they saw Jesus suddenly ascend into a cloud, and they never saw Him again. He didn't go beyond the cloud, either; He just disappeared. The cloud received Him out of their sight. Now Jesus had told them this would happen, and that it was necessary. "It is to your advantage that I go away, for if I do not go away the Counsellor will not come to you; but if I go, I will send him to you" (John 16:7). It is by means of the Spirit that Jesus makes His life available to each of us so intimately and personally

Jesus did not go to some distant planet in space. I think it is wrong to think of heaven as if it were several billion light-years away. Instead, Jesus simply stepped into a different dimension of existence—the spiritual kingdom which surrounds us on every side, invisibly. He is not far away, and neither is the throne of God and the greatness of His power. But that invisible life is imparted to us by the Holy Spirit, who came as a result of Christ's leaving this earth. Because Jesus went, I can have all of Him, and so can you.

Now the angels tell us that Christ's return is certain. "This same Jesus," they say, "will come back again." He will come in exactly the same way as they saw Him go. Just as He stepped into invisibility, He will step back again into visibility. Suddenly He will be back. And when He comes, says other Scripture, He will remove the curse from nature. Men are looking today for a solution to the ecological crisis that confronts us. How shall we solve these problems?

Well, we shall not. They will get much worse, and the crisis will get so bad that human life will actually be unable to exist any longer on the earth. Jesus said so. He said that the tribulation of those days would be so intense, so terrible, that no flesh would be saved except for the intervention of God. But when Jesus comes again He will remove the curse from nature, and nature will bloom and blossom once again. God will draw back the curtains on the exciting creation He has been working on behind the scenes throughout these twenty centuries—a new humanity. A new kind of man will suddenly be revealed. That is what Paul calls "the revealing of the sons of God" (Rom. 8:19). All the world is looking forward to this event. The hope of Christ's return is part and parcel of the mystery of incarnation, the grand strategy that God employs.

The Final Link

As the disciples turned away from the Mount of Olives, we read of the last element:

> Then they returned to Jerusalem from the mount called Olivet, which is near Jerusalem, a sabbath day's journey away; and when they had entered, they went up to the upper room, where they were staying, Peter and John and James and Andrew, Philip and Thomas, Bartholomew and Matthew, James the son of Alphaeus and Simon the Zealot and Judas the son of James. All these with one accord devoted themselves to prayer, together with the women and Mary the mother of Jesus, and with his brothers (Acts 1:12-14).

What did they do while they were waiting? Why, the only thing left to them—they prayed! Here were these men deprived of the physical presence of Jesus. The Spirit had not yet been given, so they did not have His indwelling life, but they were still not cut off from God. They were linked to Him by the marvelous communication of prayer. They gave themselves to prayer, waiting for the full revelation of what God had in mind to give them. Prayer is always an essential part of the life of the people of God. It is part of the strategy by which the incarnate Christ touches and changes the world.

Here in this introduction we have all the elements that make up the Book of Acts: a risen Lord whose life is made available through the coming of the Spirit, and who will come again in power and great glory, but with whom we are always in instant communication by means of the miracle of prayer. These elements are what enable any group of Christians to have an impact upon and to exercise a vital revolutionary force upon the age in which they live. May God grant that this will become our own experience in day-to-day living!

Chapter Two

The Birthday

Acts 1:15-2:4

As we consider the last part of Acts 1 and the first four verses of Chapter 2, it will be helpful to remember the two figures of the church in this section—a building and a body. In the last part of Chapter 1 the foundation is laid for the building, and in the first part of Chapter 2 the body is born. The scene is set for us in these verses:

> In those days Peter stood up among the brethren (the company of persons was in all about a hundred and twenty), and said, "Brethren, the scripture had to be fulfilled, which the Holy Spirit spoke beforehand by the mouth of David, concerning Judas, who was guide to those who arrested Jesus" (Acts 1:15,16).

For years I believed that these 120 believers met in the upper room, and that the Holy Spirit came upon them there. But notice that there is a break here. Although the previous paragraph does mention the upper room, (since it is part of the introduction, which ends at verse 14), it is only at verse 15 that Dr. Luke really begins to tell his story. If you link verse 15 with the last verse of the Gospel of Luke, you can see clearly where Luke takes up his narrative again. In the Gospel, Luke tells us that the disciples came back from the Mount of Olives after the ascension of Jesus and continued meeting in the courts of the temple. And that is

25

where the Pentecostal event occurred; 120 people formed much too large a group to meet in an upper room.

A Foundation of Twelve

Peter's immediate concern is that a replacement be found for Judas in the apostolic band. Judas had fallen from his place as an apostle by his betrayal of the Lord Jesus, and Peter now feels impelled by the Spirit to replace Judas. We have already seen from Paul's Letter to the Ephesians that the church is like a building, "built upon the foundation of the apostles . . ." (Eph. 2:20). It is therefore not surprising that the first thing we read about in the Book of Acts is the completing of the band of the apostles.

In the Book of Revelation John sees the city of God coming down from heaven—a beautiful picture of this magnificent church (Rev. 21:10). There is a wall around it with twelve gates, each bearing the name of one of the twelve tribes of Israel. Clearly Israel is linked to this new city. The wall also has twelve foundations, each named for one of the apostles of the Lamb. So there must also be twelve apostles. Some people think the Apostle Paul should be counted among these twelve, although Paul actually never linked himself with the twelve. Although Paul was a genuine apostle, he was not one of the twelve. Peter makes clear that Scriptures had predicted that there would be a replacement of Judas, and he quotes for us two of the Psalms to prove this. In verse 20 he says:

> For it is written in the Book of Psalms, "Let his habitation become desolate, and let there be no one to live in it" (Psa. 69:25); and "His office let another take" (Psa. 109:8).

During the ten-day period after Jesus ascended into heaven, the disciples pored over the Old Testament to see what was predicted for these days. In the Scriptures they discovered that there must be a replacement for Judas.

The Last Payment

We are also given a glimpse, in a parenthetical verse, of the tragic end of Judas. We learn how he forfeited his apostolic position:

> For he was numbered among us, and was allotted his share in this ministry. (Now this man bought a field with the reward of his wickedness; and falling headlong he burst open in the middle and all his bowels gushed out. And it became known to all the inhabitants of Jerusalem, so that the field was called in their language Akeldama, that is, Field of Blood) (Acts 1:17-19).

Here is a concise and encapsulated summary of all that happened to Judas in his last moments. When it says that he bought a field with the reward of his wickedness, it does not mean that he took the thirty pieces of silver for which he betrayed the Lord and went out and bought a field. We know from the Gospels that he took those thirty pieces of silver and threw them at the feet of the high priest, refusing to have anything to do with them. Then in what way was this Scripture fulfilled? If we put together all the references to Judas in the Gospels we learn what happened.

We are told that Judas was the treasurer of the disciples. He was so appointed by Jesus Himself. John tells us in his Gospel that Judas carried the common treasury, and also that he was a thief, and that he kept stealing money out of this common treasury (John 12:6). What for? Well, evidently Judas had accepted the current Jewish idea that when Messiah would come he would overthrow the Roman government and establish a kingdom of power and authority, with the nation of Israel at the head. Judas was feathering his nest in anticipation of this event. He had already picked a plot of ground on which he wanted to build a lovely home, and he was buying it little by little with the money which he stole from the bag. Whether he was making payments on the land or simply saving the money in order to give a cash payment at the end, we are not told. But it is likely that this is what he was doing.

As Judas realized that Jesus was approaching a crisis, he found he lacked thirty pieces of silver in order to purchase the land. So he made arrangements with the high priest to betray the Lord for those thirty pieces. But when he did the deed and led the soldiers to the Garden of Gethsemane and kissed Jesus to betray him, his eyes were apparently opened to the terrible implications of what he had done, and, wrenched with remorse and agony of conscience, he took the money back to the high priests and threw it at their feet with the words, "I have sinned in betraying innocent blood" (Matt. 27:4). Then Judas went out and hanged himself. Hanging there, on the very ground that he had hoped to buy for his home, his body bloated and swelled till the rope broke and he fell headlong, as this Scripture says, and his bowels gushed out.

Then the high priests took the thirty pieces of silver and finished paying for the property. They bought it from a potter, thus fulfilling Zechariah's prediction that this money for which Jesus would be betrayed (Zechariah had actually predicted that it would be thirty pieces of silver) would be given to the potter. Yet because this property was the scene of the suicide of Judas—a place marked by the blood of a guilty man—the high priests called it "the Field of Blood." To this day you can visit the field in Jerusalem.

Judas had to be replaced, then, in order that the church be built upon the apostles. The qualifications necessary to that replacement are given:

> So one of the men who have accompanied us during all the time that the Lord Jesus went in and out among us, beginning from the baptism of John until the day when he was taken up from us—one of these men must become with us a witness to his resurrection (Acts 1:21,22).

There were only two qualifications. The man who was chosen must have been with the apostles from the baptism of John, and he must have accompanied Jesus all through His ministry. (Remember that there were many more than twelve disciples who went around with Jesus. He chose twelve of them in order to be in a special relationship to Himself, but there were others who also accompanied Him. It was out of this larger band that a replacement would be chosen.) Not only must the replacement apostle have seen all that Jesus did, but he also must have witnessed the Lord's appearances after the resurrection. He had to give witness to the authenticity of the resurrection.

Why such stringent requirements? Well, they underscore what the New Testament is forever telling us—that our faith is not based upon myths or legends; it is based on facts and events which men have seen, felt, heard, and been involved in. This is not a "holy history," as certain theologians like to call it, a kind of pseudo-history which takes place only in the realm of ideas. No, these things actually happened, and our faith rests upon the fact that they really occurred. For this reason the apostle chosen must be able to give witness that these things were actually true.

The Lord's Decision

The process of choosing happened in an interesting place and in an interesting way:

> And they put forward two, Joseph called Barsabbas, who was surnamed Justus, and Matthias. And they prayed and said, "Lord, who knowest the hearts of all men, show which one of these two thou hast chosen to take the place in this ministry and apostleship from which Judas turned aside, to go to his own place." And they cast lots for them, and the lot fell on Matthias; and he was enrolled with the eleven apostles (Acts 1:23-26).

Evidently there were only two men out of that band of 120 who met all the qualifications for apostleship. Only two had been with Jesus the whole time and had also seen Him after the resurrection. So Justus and Matthias were put forward. The others had to decide between the two of them, and they did it in the Old Testament way: they cast lots for them. This was very much akin to what we do in flipping a coin. They may have literally used a coin, casting for heads or tails. It came up heads, and Matthias won.

Now don't misunderstand this method. It wasn't done in a casino atmosphere; it was a dignified performance. This method was used only when men were otherwise equally qualified. It indicates a recognition that God controls even the smallest things. That's why the Book of Proverbs says, "The lot is cast into the lap, but the decision is wholly from the Lord" (Prov. 16:33).

After the lot fell on Matthias he was numbered with the eleven, thereby becoming the new twelfth apostle. A subtle change occurs from here on in Acts. Up to this point the apostles are called "the eleven," but from here on they are again called "the twelve," showing that Matthias was accepted among them as a genuine apostle.

The Task of the Twelve

With the choosing of Matthias the ground was laid for the church to be built. The foundation was now poured; all the apostles were there. These mighty apostles were men who could witness to the historic foundation of Christianity.

The apostles were sent forth with a threefold task.

First, they were to be *pioneers,* going out where the name of Jesus had never been named and planting churches there. Every one of the apostles fulfilled this task. Church history tells us that Thomas went to India, Peter and Paul went to Europe, and others went to North Africa.

Second, the apostles were to be *proclaimers,* uttering what God had revealed. Remember that Jesus had said to His disciples, "I have yet many things to say to you, but you cannot bear them now" (John 16:12). He never said these "many things" in the days of His flesh; they were revealed only after the Holy Spirit came and taught these men the truths of God. That is why these apostles spoke with authority. When they spoke they did not speak as mere men, but, as Paul says, "When you received the word of God which you heard from us, you accepted it not as the word of men but as what it really is, the word of God" (1 Thes. 2:13). The apostles were proclaimers.

Finally, the apostles were *patterns*. They were intended to be examples of how the Spirit of God operates through men, penetrating a community and moving to change people and transform them. The apostles were to be examples of what a Christian ought to be. They did not live far above us; they were on the same level as we are. We are to live as the apostles lived in every way. It is in this way that these men formed the foundation of the church.

A Body is Born

As we turn to Acts 2 we find that the figure has changed. Now the church is no longer called a building, but a body. In this exciting chapter we read the account of the birth of the corporate body of Jesus Christ. Here's how the story begins:

> When the day of Pentecost had come, they were all together in one place. And suddenly a sound came from heaven like the rush of a mighty wind, and it filled all the house where they were sitting. And there appeared to them tongues as of fire, distributed and resting on each one of them. And they were all filled with the Holy Spirit and began to speak in other tongues, as the Spirit gave them utterance (Acts 2:1-4).

This passage has been subjected to much examination, and also to much abuse and distortion. We need to look at it very carefully. Three things in this passage call for our special attention. In the next chapter we will pursue the study of the subject of tongues, but right now we want to describe three other important points of the passage.

Two Loaves Into One

First, the day on which this event occurred was the Day of Pentecost. Pentecost is a Greek word which means "fifty," and the day was called that because it occurred fifty days after the Passover feast. Pentecost refers to a Jewish feast which is described in the Old Testament under the title The Feast of Weeks. Seven weeks (49 days) were to be numbered from Passover, and on the fiftieth day the Jewish people were to celebrate the Feast of Weeks, also called the Feast of the Wave Loaves. This feast came at the end of the wheat harvest in Palestine, and they were to take this new wheat, the first-fruits of the harvest, and make two loaves of it.

Now these two loaves were symbols of the two bodies from which the church was to be formed—the Jews and the Gentiles. Jesus said He came first to the lost sheep of the house of Israel, the Jews. But He also said, "I have other sheep, that are not of this fold; I must bring them also. . . . So there shall be one flock. . ." (John 10:16). He was referring to the Gentiles. Here, on the Day of Pentecost, God brought the Jews and Gentiles together and baptized them into one new body, the church.

These loaves of the Old Testament were to be baked with leaven. Leaven is yeast, and is a symbol of sin. The wave-loaf offering is the only one in the Old Testament that ever had leaven included in it. Why? Because it was God's wonderful way of telling us that the church is not made up of perfect people. It is made up of saints, but they are sinful saints. It is made up of believers who are in the process of becoming what God wants them to be, who have a divine authority and life at work inside them, changing them into the image of Christ. For this reason the loaves were baked with leaven.

Members of One Another

In this beautiful loaf symbolism lies the heart of the church. On the Day of Pentecost, right in line with this Old Testament pattern, the Holy Spirit came upon God's people. And what did He do? He took 120 people who were gathered together in one place, and made one body out of them. Here were 120 isolated individuals who had been living their lives quite separately, held together only by a mutual interest in Jesus Christ. But now they are baptized by the Spirit into one body. That is the fulfillment of Jesus' promise that when the Holy Spirit would come they would be baptized by the Spirit. The baptism of the Holy Spirit has nothing to do with any outward demonstration. It is not necessarily associated with tongues, or fire, or wind. These were the incidentals. The *essential* was the making of a body, *one* body. This was truly the birthday of the church.

When Jesus was born in Bethlehem of Judea, shepherds and wise men came to see Him, and there were angels and a star. But all these things happened only once. They never occurred in conjunction again. Likewise the wind, the fire, and the tongues occur together only once in Scripture. It is foolish to always be craving these incidentals when the Holy Spirit acts today. These are connected only with the *beginning* of the body. The only time in Scripture that we ever find the phrase "baptized with the Spirit" after this event in Acts is in First Corinthians. There the Apostle Paul says, "For by one Spirit we were all baptized into one body. . ." (1 Cor. 12:13). That is the true baptism of the Holy Spirit—"they all became one." And from then on they were part of the life of Jesus Christ and members of one another. What would happen to one would affect the others from then on. They could not be separated, they could not live their lives in isolation any longer; they were truly one body.

Certain symbols were associated with this event. There was the sound of the rush of a mighty wind; there was the appearance of tongues of fire dancing on the head of each individual; and there was the strange phenomenon of languages spoken by men who had never learned them—in other words, "tongues." What was the meaning of these symbols? They were the key to the purpose of the body. This was God's pictorial way of telling us what this new body would be like and what it would do. The first symbol was wind:

> Suddenly a sound came from heaven like the rush of a mighty wind, and it filled all the house where they were sitting (Acts 2:2).

Wind is the symbol of invisible power. Remember that Jesus said to Nicodemus that the Spirit is like the wind, which blows wherever it desires, and no one can tell where it comes from or where it will go (John 3:8). It is sovereign, mighty, powerful, irresistible, invincible. But it is also *invisible;* you can't see the wind. And this is to be a characteristic of the church. It is to be a band of men and women bound together by the life of Jesus Christ, who will accomplish great things through them when they operate in the invisible power of the Spirit. As with the wind, you cannot put your finger on their source of power, but it moves mightily to change and transform lives.

Purifying Passion

The second symbol was fire. Fire is used in two ways in the Old Testament. It is a purifier, burning up dross, garbage, and waste; and it is a symbol for enthusiasm, passion, purpose, and inner hunger. Jeremiah said, "There is in my heart. . . a burning fire" (Jer. 20:9). These two symbols indicate that there is to be within the church a yearning hunger for God which will purify the lives of those who are affected by it.

I have been challenged by the story of D. L. Moody walking down a street in New York City and thinking about a sentence he had heard: The world has yet to see what God can do with a man who is wholly yielded to him. There came into Moody's heart a great hunger, and he cried out, "O God, make me that man!" He was so filled with a sense of the overwhelming love of God that he had to go to a friend's house nearby and ask for the use of a room. For an hour or more he was caught up by this passion that had entered his heart when he became converted and which broke out from time to time with tremendous power to cleanse the evils of his life, moving him toward a unifying purpose, a relentless drive to a single goal.

That is what Luke is talking about here. When John the Baptist predicted that Jesus would come and baptize with the Holy Spirit and with fire, he meant that there would be an unexplainable passion about the church. Every Christian has felt it. We sing of it this way:

O Love that wilt not let me go,
I rest my weary soul in Thee;
I give Thee back the life I owe,
That in thine ocean depths its flow
May richer, fuller be.

Proclamation

The third symbol was the use of tongues. Certainly this was not gibberish; these were known languages spoken in that very region as well as in other places of the earth. Those who were there understood the words. The tongues were therefore edifying proclamations; they were intelligent utterances. These men were praising God in languages; the men in the audience heard the apostles telling forth the mighty works of God.

Now this is the purpose of the filling of the Spirit. It is always to enable us to speak with boldness, clarity, sincerity, and earnestness, telling forth the mighty works of God in languages that are known. There is a miracle here, no question about it, but the important point is that these men and women were seized by the Holy Spirit and filled with utterance, with proclamation. Several times in the Book of Acts it says that the disciples were filled with the Holy Spirit. But on those occasions they did not speak in other languages; they spoke in their own language. And they were filled that they might speak: "Filled with the Holy Spirit, they spoke. . . ." That is what the filling of the Spirit is for—that Christians might speak with boldness, clarity, and unction—but not always in tongues.

This is what the church should be like today. It should be filled with power, passion, and proclamation. It is exciting to see the Lord reviving His church today. All over this country and around the world there are such manifestations breaking out again. They are not spectacular, miraculous demonstrations, but outbreaks of resistless power, like a mighty wind blowing no man knows where, leading out into new ventures, new methods, new approaches, filling men with a passion and hunger for God and a reality which consumes the dross, the garbage, and the waste of our lives—a wind which impels men to speak to others about the glorious reality of a God who lives within, who is mighty and adequate in all that He does. That is the true church, the body of Christ. What an exciting thing to be a member of this living body!

Chapter Three

Beyond Tongues

Acts 2:5-21

In the phenomenon of Pentecost we see the beginning of the church of Jesus Christ, the body of Christ—in other words, the birthday of the church. Now, in the rest of Acts Chapter 2, we learn the background of the amazing sermon which the Apostle Peter preached on that occasion—a mighty sermon that brought three thousand people to Christ.

Now there were dwelling in Jerusalem Jews, devout men from every nation under heaven. And at this sound the multitude came together, and they were bewildered, because each one heard them speaking in his own language. And they were amazed and wondered, saying, "Are not all these who are speaking Galileans? And how is it that we hear, each of us in his own native language? Parthians and Medes and Elamites and residents of Mesopotamia, Judea and Cappadocia, Pontus and Asia, Phrygia and Pamphylia, Egypt and the parts of Libya belonging to Cyrene, and visitors from Rome, both Jews and proselytes, Cretans and Arabians, we hear them telling in our own tongues the mighty works of God." And all were amazed and perplexed, saying to one another, "What does this mean?" But others, mocking, said, "They are filled with new wine" (Acts 2:5-13).

Luke very carefully describes the onlookers to this amazing miracle of tongues. The tongues were intended for this certain group of people, who are described in a single phrase:

Now there were dwelling in Jerusalem Jews, *devout men from every nation under heaven* (Acts 2:5).

The holy time between Passover and Pentecost drew thousands of Jewish pilgrims from all over the earth to Jerusalem. Josephus, the Jewish historian of this time, tells us that the city of Jerusalem (which normally had a population of 50,000) would often be swollen in numbers to well over a million. It was to this multitude that the miracle of Pentecost was directed.

God summoned the throngs with the sound of a mighty rushing wind. "At this sound the multitude came together" (Acts 2:6). The "sound" does not refer to the sound of tongues (that would hardly be loud enough to attract the attention of the whole city and countryside!) but to the mighty rush of wind that attracted people from all over the city. It is the same word that occurs in verse 2: "And suddenly a sound came from heaven. . . ." God, as it were, turned on a siren to bring the people together!

No Interpreters Needed

When the people heard this great sound they came rushing together into the temple, but when they arrived they were still more bewildered, "because each one heard them speaking in his own language." They heard the strange sound of certain men and women, evidently peasants from Galilee, who were speaking in over sixteen different languages. It was quite evident that these people were not educated. And this was long before the days of the art of linguistics, so it was very difficult to learn a foreign language. You had to live in a country in order to learn its language. Yet these untrained men and women were speaking in languages which were foreign to them.

Notice that no special supernatural activity was required to understand the languages. These pilgrims were amazed that they could hear these utterance in their own native tongues. Luke even names the localities and therefore the different languages that were being spoken. Beginning with the East, he lists a group of dialects east of Jerusalem spoken by Parthians, Medes, Elamites, and residents of Mesopotamia. Then he moves north, including Judea (where they were), Cappadocia, Pontus, Asia, Phrygia, and Pamphylia—all Roman provinces of Asia Minor, as we know it today. Then he moves south to Egypt and the parts of Libya belonging to Cyrene, in northern Africa, then west to Rome and Crete, and then south again to Arabia.

Although the apostles were speaking in different languages, they were all saying the same things. They were declaring, literally, the "magnificences of God." They were praising God. They were not preaching the gospel; they were speaking of how great God is, worshiping and praising God. That was the phenomenon that arrested the attention of this great multitude as they came pressing into the temple courts.

Curiosity and Ridicule

In Luke's record of the crowd's reaction, there are two words he uses for astonishment: "amazed" and "bewildered." Twice he indicates that they were amazed. The literal translation from Greek is "to push out of their senses." Or, in the modern phrase, "it blew their minds." Linked with that, Luke says, they were bewildered. The word is really one which means they were hit hard, stunned; they were staggered by this amazing thing, especially since they easily recognized the languages they heard.

Then we have two more words that indicate puzzlement. They "wondered," and they were "perplexed." Those are suggestive words. "Wondered" means they sought for a solution. "What is behind all this? Why is this happening?" The second word, "perplexed," means literally "thoughts running through their minds." Two more expressions that are recorded of this crowd are especially interesting. When the human mind is confronted with a startling new thing it reacts in one of two ways, as in this case. First, some people began to inquire, representing the group of open minds that are always ready to investigate further before coming to a conclusion. But the other group immediately dismissed the phenomenon with the infantile reaction of mockery and ridicule. They looked at the disciples and said, "They're drunk! That explains it. They've been getting into the new wine!"

Explaining Reality

All this sets the stage for Peter's explanation, and in the next few verses we have a wonderful message delivered by the Apostle on this occasion:

> But Peter, standing with the eleven, lifted up his voice and addressed them, "Men of Judea and all who dwell in Jerusalem, let this be known to you, and give ear to my words. For these men are not drunk, as you suppose, since it is only the third hour of the day; but this is what was spoken by the prophet Joel" (Acts 2:14-16).

Notice how alert Peter was. Led by the Holy Spirit, he immediately began to speak. And he spoke so effectively that he never got a chance to give an altar call (a wonderful thing to have happen!) because he stated the truth in the power of the Spirit. That was Peter's message—a simple explanation of reality. The preaching of the gospel is an explanation of what things are really like. Peter seized this occasion to make clear what lay behind the supernatural events of the Day of Pentecost. His message contained three parts—an explanation of the phenomenon of tongues, a declaration of Jesus of Nazareth, and an application to the crowd. Right now let's discuss Peter's explanation of the phenomenon of tongues.

First of all, what Peter said to the crowd when he stood up was not quite what we read in the Revised Standard Version— "For these men are not drunk, as you suppose." What the Greek literally says is, "He stood up and said to them, 'Not as you suppose are these men drunk.' " In other words, they *are* drunk, but not from new wine; rather, it is what Joel said would happen—the Spirit of God has come upon them. It is true that to be controlled by the Holy Spirit does affect a person somewhat like alcohol does. Paul implies this in Ephesians: "Do not get drunk with wine. . . but be filled with the Spirit" (Eph. 5:18). But Peter says, "No, it is only nine o'clock in the morning. Everyone knows that hardly anyone drinks before eleven o'clock, so it can't be that they're drunk with new wine; they're drunk with the Holy Spirit!"

In the Last Days

And then he quotes this amazing passage from the prophet Joel:

And in the last days it shall be, God declares, that I will pour out my Spirit upon all flesh, and your sons and your daughters shall prophesy, and your young men shall see visions, and your old men shall dream dreams; yea, and on my menservants and my maidservants in those days I will pour out my Spirit; and they shall prophesy. And I will show wonders in the heaven above and signs on the earth beneath, blood and fire and vapor of smoke; the sun shall be turned into darkness and the moon into blood, before the day of the Lord comes, the great and manifest day. And it shall be that whoever calls on the name of the Lord shall be saved (Acts 2:17-21).

Peter's explanation is very simple. Since this is exactly what Joel declared would happen, it is therefore neither unexpected nor unexplained. The key to this passage from Joel is the phrase "I will pour out my Spirit upon *all flesh.* " If you read the prophecy as it occurs in the second chapter of Joel, you will find that in the words preceding this passage the prophet had predicted that the Lord would visit His people. He would come to them and live in their midst. Then, as the prophet puts it, "afterward" (after this visitation) "I will pour out my Spirit upon all flesh." A distinction is made between the visitation of God to Israel and the pouring out of the Spirit upon all peoples everywhere—Gentiles as well as Jews. The emphasis of this section is that now the good news about Jesus Christ is to go out to the Gentiles as well as to the Jews.

Now Peter announces that the time has come when God will pour out His Spirit upon all flesh, Jews and Gentiles alike—not only all people everywhere, but all kinds of people: "Your sons and your daughters shall prophesy, and your young men shall see visions" (Acts 2:17). Note the emphasis upon youth. God is saying that in this age of the Spirit, leadership, effectiveness, and power will not be limited to gray hairs; young men and women will also speak and lead, will also prophesy and see visions. Even upon servants, obscure people, and insignificant people will God pour out His Spirit, and they too will prophesy.

What Peter did *not* say is as important as what he *did* say. He did *not* say, "*Thus is fulfilled* what was said by the prophet Joel." From other Scriptures we learn that Joel's prophecy has yet to be fulfilled in its ultimate meaning. God will again visit His people at the second return of Jesus Christ. Then, after His return, the Spirit will once more be poured out. When Peter quotes this passage he changes the word "afterward" to the phrase "in the last days." Peter adapts Joel's prediction to the present age of the Spirit, which begins, he says, with the pouring out of the Spirit of God.

It is also important to notice that in this quotation of Joel there is no mention at all of tongues; instead, Joel refers to another gift of the Spirit, the gift of prophecy. Prophecy is the ability to declare or tell forth the Word of God in power. Young men and old, servants and obscure people will all be equipped by the Spirit to tell forth the Word of God with power. That will be the mark of the age, Joel says. The emphasis is not upon tongues at all—not even upon gifts—but upon the Spirit who gives the gifts.

The last section of the prophecy was not fulfilled on the Day of Pentecost. According to the prophecy of Jesus Himself, this is yet for the future (Matt. 24:29). The day is coming when God will show signs on earth and in the heaven above: blood and fire and vapor of smoke.

The sun shall be turned into darkness and the moon into blood, before the day of the Lord comes, the great and manifest day (Acts 2:20).

Thus Peter gives us the great parenthesis which marks the age of the Spirit in which we live. It began on Pentecost, and it will end after the Great Tribulation, but through it all runs one great unbroken thread:

And it shall be that whoever calls on the name of the Lord shall be saved (Acts 2:21).

It is an age of faith, an age of belief. When men believe what God has said and call upon the name of the Lord, asking Jesus to be Lord of their life, they are filled with the Spirit. There need be no manifestation, no outward signs. It will be just as Jesus Himself said:

On the last day of the feast, the great day, Jesus stood up and proclaimed, "If anyone thirst, let him come to me and drink. He who believes in me, as the scripture has said, 'Out of his heart shall flow rivers of living water' " (John 7:37,38).

John immediately adds,

Now this he said about the Spirit, which those who believe in him were to receive. . . (John 7:39).

From the Day of Pentecost on, the Spirit is given to *everyone* who believes in the Lord Jesus Christ. That is the reason for the manifestations on the Day of Pentecost.

Is It the Same Gift?

Now the question comes, what about today's manifestation of tongues? Today many people are saying, "We are experiencing a second Pentecost. There is a new outpouring of the Holy Spirit. It is the 'latter rain' that was predicted by Joel to follow the 'early rain' of Pentecost." But no one seems to have noticed that Joel says that the latter rain will occur only *after* the second return of Jesus Christ—not before. Well, then, what about this modern experience of "speaking in tongues"? How should we evaluate it?

The great question that needs to be answered is whether or not the modern phenomenon is the same gift as that recorded in the Bible. We are exhorted by John to "test the spirits, to see whether they are of God" (1 John 4:1). The only way we can know for sure is to understand exactly what the marks of the Biblical gift are and then to compare these with what we see today.

Whenever the true gift of tongues is manifested it will always be characterized in four ways. The Holy Spirit always moves in line with the Word of God. First, as we have clearly seen, the Biblical gift of tongues *always* consists of known languages, spoken somewhere on earth. They may be unknown to the immediate audience hearing them (as in the fourteenth chapter of First Corinthians), but they are spoken somewhere.

Second, Biblical tongues are addressed to God as praise and worship. The early Christians *did not preach the gospel* in tongues; they *praised and worshiped God* in these strange languages. Paul confirms this with these words: "For one who speaks in a tongue speaks not to men but to God" (1 Cor. 14:2).

The third mark of true Biblical tongues is very clear in this Pentecostal incident. The gift of tongues is intended to be manifested publicly—never privately. Again Paul confirms this when he says, "To each is given the manifestation of the Spirit for the common good" (1 Cor. 12:7). The gifts are not for *private blessing;* they are for the *common good.* In First Corinthians 14 Paul insists that if tongues are nevertheless exercised in the church, they *must* be interpreted, lest they be of no value whatsoever. Tongues were never intended for the benefit of the speaker, but for the edifying of the hearers. The miracle at Pentecost occurred for the benefit of the thousands of Jews who had gathered at Jerusalem from the four corners of the earth.

This leads to the last mark of Biblical tongues, which is also clearly evident at Pentecost and which is definitely referred to by Paul in First Corinthians 14. The Biblical gift of tongues is a sign to unbelievers, and not to believers. Paul quotes an Old Testament prophet, the prophet Isaiah, who predicted that one day God would send to Israel men who spoke in strange tongues (Isa. 28:11,12). "And," says Isaiah, "when you hear these you will know that the hour has struck when God will send His message out to all peoples everywhere." The tongues of Pentecost were therefore a sign to unbelievers that the gospel was now going out to the whole Gentile world. Wherever you find tongues occurring in the New Testament you always find unbelievers present, because tongues were a sign to them rather than to the believers.

The Need for Warning

That is what the Biblical gift of tongues was like. In my judgment, the present-day manifestation is definitely not the same thing, since it doesn't meet the Biblical standard at all. Furthermore, we need to recognize that the utterance of strange syllables is a very common thing in other religions, occurring frequently in Hinduism and several African cults. Long before Christ, Plato and the early Greek philosophers discussed the phenomenon of speaking in strange syllables under religious ecstasy. But in my opinion this has nothing to do with the Biblical gift of languages; it is something else. At best, it is a psychological response, fulfilling an overpowering desire to have something that will mark a person as unusually favored in God's sight. This is almost always the explanation behind the hunger of those who seek this gift.

The false gift often appears in connection with a genuine moving of the Holy Spirit, and sometimes it is hard to separate the true from the false. This false gift is often a seed planted by the enemy in the midst of a genuine moving of the Spirit, and much of the blessing that comes from the genuine awakening is unthinkingly attributed to tongues. But it is clear to me that the results of yielding to this false gift of tongues is frequently spiritual derailment. Many who have begun well, who have begun to walk in the Spirit, are derailed—shunted into a dead-end street which never goes anywhere. It ultimately results in divisiveness, in separation of Christian from Christian, as well as in prolonged barrenness in the spiritual life. That is why there is need for a warning: the true gift of God will always be in line with the Biblical picture.

We need to take special heed to Peter's final word in this section, that in this age of the Spirit all that the Spirit of God has for us is given to whomever calls on the name of the Lord. As Paul says in the opening words of his Letter to the Ephesians, "Blessed be the God and Father. . . who has blessed us in Christ with every spiritual blessing in the heavenly places" (Eph. 1:3). And Peter adds, "His divine power *has granted* to us all things that pertain to life and godliness" (2 Pet. 1:3). We need nothing further, no new provision or supply; we only need to claim by faith what is already ours in Christ Jesus.

Chapter Four

Confrontation

Acts 2:22-37

Peter said that the age of the Spirit would begin with proclamation and end with tribulation. We are two thousand years away from the beginning of that age, and therefore two thousand years closer to the end. In fact, it may well be that the end has already begun. Twenty-five years ago, many people would not have believed that the Book of Revelation could be literally fulfilled, exactly as written. But the Apostle Peter said that throughout this whole age the good news would be that whoever would call upon the name of the Lord would be saved; they would be free from everything that keeps them from being the kind of men and women they were intended to be. Salvation is a restoration to what God intended when he made man in the first place. And the way they will be saved, Peter says, is to call upon the name of the Lord.

But having said that, he is ready to spring a bomb on these people. The Lord upon whom men must call, Peter now announces, is none other than the Prophet who was crucified fifty days ago right here in the city of Jerusalem: Jesus of Nazareth. This stunning announcement fell upon the ears of these people with fantastic power. Peter set before them a threefold argument that began with the humanity of Jesus and ended with a clear proclamation of His deity. Peter moved with such precision and such irrefutable proofs that, when he arrived at his conclusion, three thousand people arrived with him.

The first movement is the foundation of facts:

> Men of Israel, hear these words: Jesus of Nazareth, a man attested to you by God with mighty works and wonders and signs which God did through him in your midst, as you yourselves know—this Jesus, delivered up according to the definite plan and foreknowledge of God, you crucified and killed by the hands of lawless men. But God raised him up, having loosed the pangs of death, because it was not possible for him to be held by it (Acts 2:22-24).

These are the great events in history upon which our Christian faith rests: the life and the death and the resurrection of the Lord Jesus Christ. These are historical events which would have been recorded in any daily newspaper of the time. If these events did not occur, Christianity is nothing but a hoax—a bad joke. It is upon the historicity of these events that our faith must rest. If they had not occurred, who would know better than Peter's audience? These people had been in Jerusalem throughout the time that these events took place. They had been in the city when it was so stirred with the arrest and trial and death of Jesus. Of all people in the world, Peter's listeners would have been best able to contradict the Apostle if any of these events were legend or myth. But the Apostle simply sets forth these facts as conclusive evidence and indisputable proofs to support the claims of the Christian faith.

The Standard Man

Each of these events is designed to teach mankind some important truth. The first is the pattern of normal humanity which Jesus set before us. He was a man, says Peter; he was not a specter or a phantom, nor was He a superman. He was a normal man, authenticated and approved by God as a standard of humanity. When you see Jesus you see what God intended man to be. He is the standard man. He pleased God because He was what God wanted men to be.

God's method of authentication was by "mighty works and

wonders and signs," the miracles of Jesus. These amazing miracles of changing water to wine, of stilling the winds and the waves, of multiplying the loaves and fishes, of healing the sick, casting out demons, and raising the dead are simply manifestations of man's intended control over nature. These signs were not done by Jesus because He was God. They were done by a man who was yielded to the indwelling power and life of God within. And by means of that power Jesus did these great miracles. That is the normal pattern of humanity, the means by which the life of God the Father was made available to the Man Jesus.

Jesus was indeed God—there is no question about that—but that was not the secret of His ministry. The secret of Jesus' ministry was that He was a Man through whom God worked. God wants to communicate to us through the life of Jesus in the Gospels, to tell us to act and think and react as Jesus did, for He is the pattern of normal humanity.

Putting Evil to Death

The second step in Peter's argument is to focus on the death of Jesus, in which is revealed the purpose of God in history:

> This Jesus, delivered up according to the definite plan and foreknowledge of God, you crucified and killed by the hands of lawless men (Acts 2:23).

The death of Jesus was accomplished, Peter said, by you Jews at the hands of Roman Gentiles, who were lawless in regard to the observance of God's law. Although you did this, Peter continued, your murder nevertheless fulfilled the determinate program and plan of God. The Cross was no accident in the life of Jesus—it was an essential event, programmed by God the Father from the beginning of time. Peter indicates here that the only way God could deal with the problem of human evil—the basic problem—was by the death of Jesus. It had to happen, and God arranged it. There is no way to deal with this evil within us except by death.

We are all capable of putting on a respectable front. But within us all lurks an evil, reactionary nature which responds with all the ugly things that afflict us today. We are all capable of such evil. Even at moments when we want to do good we find this evil nature coming out. This is what God is aiming at destroying.

ILLUS

A young man came to see me, a man whom I had not seen for a number of years. He told me about his life, how he had gotten into difficulties and spent a few years in prison. Now he was really sorry for some of the things he had done, and he realized he was miserable and had made a fool of himself, and he wanted to straighten out his life. We talked about what it would take to correct his life, and about the need of a restoration to the love and fellowship of the Lord Jesus. Then we prayed together. Yet that very night this young man went to the place where he worked, cleaned out the till, and took off with $200 of his father's money. The possibilities of evil are in all of us. God says that the only way this sinful nature can be broken is by the death of Jesus; there is no other way out.

When Peter speaks about the definite plan and foreknowledge of God, he is not saying that the men and women who were involved in the death of Jesus were robots, automatons who could not help themselves; that though they had to put Jesus to death they could hardly be blamed, since they were operating according to the predetermined program of God. What was determined was that, once having made a choice to reject God, they no longer had a choice as to *how* that rejection would be manifested. It must manifest itself in some deliberate action and attitude against Jesus Christ.

Not One Challenge

Now Peter moves to the third point—the resurrection:

But God raised him up, having loosed the pangs of death, because it was not possible for him to be held by it (Acts 2:24).

The resurrection power of God, a power which man cannot duplicate, is revealed here. The ability to bring life out of death, to correct a situation that is hopeless, to change a person's hardened heart—that is resurrection power. A high school boy was telling me how baffled his father was by his son's conversion. He couldn't understand it; it fit no psychological pattern that he knew of. He couldn't explain why his son was suddenly so different. And because he couldn't explain it, it angered him and he fought it all the way. People who come into contact with the resurrection power of God frequently react this way.

Mankind is always dreaming of finding a way to beat death. One of the more ghastly propositions today is to put yourself in a condition of deep-freeze if you have an incurable disease, until science has found a cure, maybe fifty or a hundred years from now. Then doctors will thaw you out, and you will get a chance to go on living. What a miserable thing! What a far cry from resurrection life! This is not what happened to Jesus Christ when He rose from the dead in all the fulness and vitality of His person.

The strange and remarkable thing about Peter's sermon is that not a single voice was lifted in protest. To me one of the greatest proofs of the resurrection of Jesus is that Peter could stand up in the city where these events had taken place a little more than a month before and tell these people that Jesus had risen from the dead, with not a single person challenging him. They knew that the authorities could not produce the body of Jesus, though they would have given a king's ransom to be able to do so. The people had heard all the wild rumors of Jesus appearing alive to His own disciples, and now they stand in mute and stricken silence as the Apostle drives home with powerful strokes the sword of the Spirit, convicting them of the truth of his claim.

Pointing Toward Jesus

The second major movement in Peter's address was to reveal the background of the resurrection prediction. Behind the actual events of the resurrection lay a pattern of prediction which tremendously enhanced the power of the Apostle's argument. He quotes now from David:

> For David says concerning him, "I saw the Lord always before me, for he is at my right hand that I may not be shaken; therefore my heart was glad, and my tongue rejoiced; moreover my flesh will dwell in hope. For thou wilt not abandon my soul to Hades, nor let thy Holy One see corruption. Thou hast made known to me the ways of life; thou wilt make me full of gladness with thy presence" (Acts 2:25-28).

The point that Peter is making here by quoting from the sixteenth Psalm is not merely that David had predicted that Jesus would rise from the dead, but also that David had declared that the resurrection was absolutely essential in view of the life that Jesus had lived. Peter's whole argument hangs on this "therefore" in verse 26. Before that, David foresaw Jesus as saying, "I saw the Lord always before me, for he is at my right hand that I may not be shaken." His would be a life lived continually in dependence on the power and authority of the Father. "Therefore [because I will rest in trust upon God] my heart was glad, and my tongue rejoiced; moreover my flesh will rest in hope. "For," he goes on, "you will not abandon my soul to Hades, and you will not let my body rot in the grave. Instead, you will make known to me the ways of life, and in your presence will be fullness of gladness and joy."

That prediction of David indicates that the kind of life which Jesus lived guaranteed that death would have no power over Him. In the words of Major Ian Thomas, "He had to be what He was in order to do what He did." And then Major Thomas continues, "He had to do what He did in order that we might have what He is. And we must have what He is in order to be what He was." That is Christianity.

The second point that Peter makes here is that David was not talking about himself:

> Brethren, I may say to you confidently of the patriarch David that he both died and was buried, and his tomb is with us to

this day. Being therefore a prophet, and knowing that God had sworn with an oath to him that he would set one of his descendants upon his throne, he foresaw and spoke of the resurrection of the Christ, that he was not abandoned to Hades, nor did his flesh see corruption. This Jesus God raised up, and of that we all are witnesses (Acts 2:29-32).

Skeptics say that these predictive psalms, such as Psalms 16 and 22, reflect only some personal experience that the psalmist was going through, and that it is wrong to read them as pointing forward to Jesus Christ. But notice how Peter denies that argument. He says, "In the sixteenth Psalm David is talking about a man whose body does not rot in the grave. Now that couldn't be David, because David died and was buried. And if you don't believe it, there's his tomb."

Peter's third point in his sermon is that death had no effect whatever upon Jesus Christ. Some Christians accept the theory that when Jesus died His soul went to hell, where He preached to the spirits that were in hades and led some of them captive up to heaven. But Jesus did not go to hades; He did not go to hell. As He said when He died, "Father, into thy hands I commit my spirit" (Luke 23:46). The argument of the Apostle was, then, that death had *no* power over Him—none at all. It could touch neither His soul nor His body.

Evidence of Lordship

In the last movement of Peter's sermon we see the demonstration of the results:

"Being therefore exalted at the right hand of God, and having received from the Father the promise of the Holy Spirit, he has poured out this which you see and hear. For David did not ascend into the heavens; but he himself says, 'The Lord said to my Lord, Sit at my right hand, till I make thy enemies a stool for thy feet.' Let all the house of Israel therefore know assuredly that God has made him both Lord and Christ, this Jesus whom you crucified." Now when they heard this they were cut to the heart, and said to Peter and the rest of the apostles, "Brethren, what shall we do?" (Acts 2:33-37).

Once again the Apostle turned his whole audience into witnesses of his claim. He says, "You're just now seeing the proof of what David had predicted would happen." And then he quotes Psalm 110, in which God says to David's Lord, "Sit at my right hand until I make you ruler over all, till I make your enemies your footstool." And Peter says that this has now happened—that the tongues of fire, the sound of the mighty wind, and the utterance of the strange languages were proof that Jesus of Nazareth is Lord and Christ.

"Lord" means Ruler of all things, King over all men, the One who holds the key to life and death, heaven and hell. There is no authority or power that exists that does not take its direction and its limitation from Him. "Christ" means Messiah. "Jesus" is His name; "Christ" is His title. Christ means Messiah, the Promised One, the Deliverer, the only hope that mankind has ever had.

Suddenly all of this made fantastic sense to the multitude. The full force of Peter's arguments thudded home, and they realized that they were in a very precarious position. This One whom Peter had proved by indisputable evidence to be Lord was the very person they had crucified fifty days before. They were cut to the heart, and they cried out, "Brethren, what shall we do?"

It is here that Christianity rests its case. Jesus Christ is Lord whether men know it or not. The very forces that control their lives are dependent upon Him. The declaration of Peter on this day was that Jesus is the inevitable Man. There is no way you can avoid Him. He is Lord over all things, and sooner or later you have to deal with Jesus Christ, whether you like it or not; you have no option.

Chapter Five

The Essential Ingredients

Acts 2:37-47

The response to Peter's message on the Day of Pentecost was similar to the remarkable awakening that recently swept across our country, especially on college campuses. It is an awakening in which the wife of a college president gets up in chapel and confesses her antagonism toward both the school and the town, confessing that she had not enjoyed her years there and had held it against the whole college community. As she confesses, she tells of God's dealing with her and of the warm love and acceptance He has now given her toward both the town and the school. At the end of her testimony, it is like the Day of Pentecost. People swarm to the altar, cut to the heart because of what they have heard.

That is exactly what happened two thousand years ago, confirming that we are living in the same age of the Spirit that was begun on the Day of Pentecost. Continuing in Acts 2, we read:

> Now when they heard this they were cut to the heart, and said to Peter and the rest of the apostles, "Brethren, what shall we do?" (Acts 2:37).

To be cut to the heart is to be deeply convicted, to have a sense of personal involvement in what has been said and an awareness of the tremendous impact of revealed truth. These people had had their eyes opened. They began to realize that behind all the normal events of everyday life was the power of God. And now

55

they understood that the Man they had nailed to a cross some fifty days earlier was the very God of power Himself.

In fear and perhaps despair the crowd cried out, "Men and brethren, what shall we do?" This is the work of the Spirit of God, making men aware of the Lordship of Jesus. Jesus is Lord. By Him all things consist and are held together. When we understand that Jesus is the inescapable One, there comes this deep sense of conviction, of being cut to the heart.

Change Your Mind

Peter responds by providing a crystal-clear explanation of how to become a Christian:

> And Peter said to them, "Repent, and be baptized, every one of you, in the name of Jesus Christ for the forgiveness of your sins, and you shall receive the gift of the Holy Spirit. For the promise is to you and to your children and to all that are far off, every one whom the Lord our God calls to him." And he testified with many other words and exhorted them, saying, "Save yourselves from this crooked generation" (Acts 2:38-40).

There are two things you need to do, Peter says, and then there is one thing God will do. First you need to *repent*—a word which is greatly misunderstood. Feeling sorry and crying may go along with repentance, but such emotions do not necessarily mean that you have repented. To repent (Greek *metanoia*) means to change your mind. You have been thinking that everything was all right with you—but now you must think again. You have been thinking that Jesus may have been a great teacher, or a great prophet, but that He is not the Son of God—but now you must think again. Peter is saying, "Get in tune with reality, line up with things the way they really are!"

A New Beginning

The second thing to do is to be baptized. Baptism does not make you magically clean, but it is the outward and symbolic declaration of the change of mind that you have experienced inside. Baptism is an open identification with Jesus Christ. It is a cutting off from the old way of thinking, a beginning of a new life. Among these Jews baptism was a very clearly understood process. When a Gentile became a Jew, his body was washed all over, and that was a symbol that he was beginning a new life, starting all over again. That is what baptism basically means.

But perhaps you are saying, "Wait a minute. Peter says, 'Be baptized in the name of Christ for the forgiveness of sins.' " It is often taught that when you are baptized your sins are forgiven. But the Greek construction here can also be translated, "Be baptized in the Name of Jesus Christ because of the forgiveness of your sins." A little later in Acts the Apostle Peter says to another crowd of people in the house of Cornelius, "Everyone who believes in him receives forgiveness of sins through his name" (Acts 10:43). Baptism is not the important thing here. It is *repentance and belief in His name* that obtains remission of sins. It is changing your mind about Jesus Christ that enables God to wipe out all your guilt and all the sins of your past.

When that happens, Peter says, you will receive the Holy Spirit. That is, God the third Person will come and live inside you. And His work will be to make Jesus Christ visible, real, and close to you—to impart His life to your own. Notice that Peter did not promise these people the gift of tongues, flames of fire, or a sound of rushing wind. The Holy Spirit came with these phenomena as symbols of what the whole age of the Spirit would be like, but they are not promised to every individual. The Spirit of God comes into the human heart without any demonstration or sign at all, on the basis of changed minds. And on this basis these people received the promise of the Father.

God's Choice, Our Choice

The Apostle goes on to say that this promise is available to everyone:

For the promise is to you and to your children and to all that

are far off, everyone whom the Lord our God calls to him
(Acts 2:39).

Notice that the promise is to those whom God calls. That remarkable statement indicates that we do not really find God; He
finds us. If you have a hunger to know God, and you think it
started with you, you are mistaken. It started with God. God the
Father is working within you, drawing you, calling you. Yet, as
Peter goes on, he links this truth with a decision of the will:

> And he testified with many other words and exhorted them,
> saying, "Save yourselves from this crooked generation" (Acts
> 2:40).

Peter's entire message is not recorded here, but we have this
summary: "Save yourselves from this crooked generation." He is
saying that *you* have to do something. The call of God alone is
not enough. You have to make a decision to become identified
with Jesus Christ. And the minute you do that, God gives you the
gift of the Holy Spirit.

To Experience Life

We see the immediate results of that decision at Pentecost in
these verses:

> So those who received his word were baptized, and there were
> added that day about three thousands souls. And they devoted
> themselves to the apostles' teaching and fellowship, to the
> breaking of bread and the prayers (Acts 2:41,42).

In this brief paragraph we have the four fundamentals of Christian growth. If you have received Jesus Christ into your heart, the
whole of Christian life lies ahead for you to experience. First, be
baptized, as these people were. Imagine the effect on the city of
Jerusalem when these three thousand people openly identified
themselves with the despised Nazarene. No wonder a great
awakening broke out in Jerusalem! The second fundamental of
the Christian life is teaching: "They devoted themselves to the

apostles' teaching." These mighty apostles were commissioned by the Lord Jesus, by the power of the Holy Spirit, to tell us the truth about life. The only hope we have of working out our problems is to begin to understand the apostles' teaching. And this teaching was the Word of God, the Scriptures.

Next, these new followers of Christ devoted themselves to fellowship, which means holding all things in common, sharing together. Here are three thousand people, many of whom had come from other parts of the world into Jerusalem for that occasion, and who did not know each other. But now that they are one in Christ, they begin to love each other, to share their burdens and needs with one another, and to pray together. There was a wonderful sense of community, of common-ness, of belonging to each other. That is the intended life for the body of Christ. God has designed that His life should be manifest through a body. And if the body is not operating, then the power of the life of God is not manifest.

Forgiving One Another

The Apostle Paul says, "Do not grieve the Holy Spirit of God." And then he lists the things that grieve the Spirit!

Let all bitterness and wrath and anger and clamor and slander be put away from you, with all malice, and be kind to one another, tenderhearted, forgiving one another, as God in Christ forgave you (Eph. 4:31,32).

If this is not happening, the Spirit of God is grieved. And when He is grieved, He does not act. There is no life. The church becomes dull and sterile, manifesting only a lifeless ritual. Fellowship is not an option for Christians; it is an essential. That is why when the Holy Spirit of God begins to move in any congregation or assembly of Christians He first begins to heal the brokenness of human relationships, getting people to admit to each other their malice, their anger, their frustration, and their grudges—and to forgive one another. That is when life begins to flow once again through the body of the Lord Jesus Christ.

The fourth element in a vital Christian experience is worship. The new Christians in Acts broke bread and prayed together. In the breaking of bread Luke is undoubtedly referring not merely to their meals; he is talking about their sharing together in that symbolic testimony to the basis of Christian life, the life and death of the Lord Jesus—in other words, communion. In the breaking of bread and praying together we are related to God; we speak to God and are identified with Him.

Fear and Favor

In the last paragraph of Acts 2 we have a beautiful picture of the practical effects of Christianity upon the world all around, upon the church within, and even toward God Himself:

> And fear came upon every soul; and many wonders and signs were done through the apostles. And all who believed were together and had all things in common; and they sold their possessions and goods and distributed them to all, as any had need. And day by day, attending the temple together and breaking bread in their homes, they partook of food with glad and generous hearts, praising God and having favor with all the people. And the Lord added to their number day by day those who were being saved (Acts 2:43-47).

The first effect, fear, was upon the surrounding world. Why this fear? Well, suddenly everyone who was in that city at this time saw that God was working through these people. The supernatural was very visible, and it baffled them. A power that was more than human was obviously at work, a power that was manifest in wonders and signs—in miracles. Today many people feel that we have to recapture this wonderful age and reproduce these marvelous miracles and signs. But this is where God always *begins* when He meets with men. Because unregenerate men are by and large confined to a world of visible things, believing only what they can see, God in His condescending grace begins at that level. But the things which He does in the realm of the spiritual are actually far greater than those which He does in the realm of the physical. As His church grows, God moves from the physical level into the deepest level of humanity. It is in the *spirit* of man, through God's transforming grace, that the mightiest manifestation of His power is found.

The second effect of the Spirit's work is within the church:

> And all who believed were together and had all things in common; and they sold their possessions and goods and distributed them to all, as any had need (Acts 2:44,45).

This passage is not a blueprint for a new government or a new economic system. These believers simply established a common fund, from which the needy among them were helped. To do it, some of them sold some property and gave up some of the things they owned to the fund. And that is Christianity in action—to be always concerned about the needy.

The last result of the Spirit's work is the glory that a practical Christianity brings to God:

> And day by day, attending the temple together and breaking bread in their homes, they partook of food with glad and generous hearts, praising God and having favor with all the people. And the Lord added to their number day by day those who were being saved (Acts 2:46,47).

Here God is obviously at work, being glorified in the midst of His people and being worshipped and praised by them. Christianity lived in this way by the body resulted in a continuous response on the part of the people around them. This is also what we are seeing today, as the Holy Spirit continues to make the Father known to all, Jew and Gentile alike. The same vitality that was evident among the new believers in those days is being seen again today—the vitality that comes only from a life lived in the strength of the Spirit of God.

Chapter Six

The Healing Hand of Jesus

Acts 3:1-10

We have no complete record of all the wonders and signs that were done through the apostles in the opening period of the new church, but we do have this story of the lame man who was healed at the Beautiful Gate of the temple. Luke evidently selected this healing out of a number of miracles that occurred in order to teach us something very significant. For this reason we should give it our careful attention.

Now Peter and John were going up to the temple at the hour of prayer, the ninth hour. And a man lame from birth was being carried, whom they laid daily at that gate of the temple which is called Beautiful to ask alms of those who entered the temple. Seeing Peter and John about to go into the temple, he asked for alms. And Peter directed his gaze at him, with John, and said, "Look at us." And he fixed his attention upon them, expecting to receive something from them. But Peter said, "I have no silver and gold, but I give you what I have; in the name of Jesus Christ of Nazareth, walk." And he took him by the right hand and raised him up; and immediately his feet and ankles were made strong. And leaping up he stood and walked and entered the temple with them, walking and leaping and praising God (Acts 3:1-8).

As Peter and John went up to the temple according to their custom, they found a lame man there. It is interesting to note that Peter and John were still going to the temple in order to meet with the other believers. Evidently they still gathered in the temple court where Jesus used to teach, and they were meeting there for prayer and study, for fellowship and the breaking of bread. They had not yet forsaken the temple.

Later, in the Book of Hebrews, these early Christians were exhorted to leave the temple, since the temple was no longer the significant meetingplace of God with man. The temple in Jerusalem was just a building, and already these Christians were learning that God had designed a living temple, and that the temple of stone was merely a symbol of the real temple—the human body—where God intended to meet man. "You are God's temple," Paul wrote, "and God wants to meet you inside of you, where you live, down at the deepest part." But here in Acts there is no immediate breaking off from the symbolic temple. God is patient and understanding with His people, and He knows that we learn slowly.

As Peter and John were going up to the temple it was the ninth hour, or three o'clock in the afternoon. This was the usual time of prayer for the Jews, but it also had special significance to the Christians. It was at three o'clock in the afternoon that Jesus had died on the Cross; it was at that hour that He had cried in a loud voice, "It is finished," bowing His head and delivering up His spirit.

On their way into the temple the two apostles met this man who had been lame from birth. It has always been a puzzle to me why this man had not been healed by Jesus. He had apparently been brought to the temple regularly for a long, long time, and Jesus must certainly have seen him as he passed into the temple. But He never healed him. I think this indicates that God has His time for great events, and that until that time things sometimes go on pretty much as usual. At any rate, this lame man was waiting at the gate of the temple. The striking thing about this story is that when he asked alms of Peter, Peter stopped and said to him, "Look at us." This is right in line with the method of Jesus. He never just walked up to someone and healed him without first directing his attention to Himself. Like Peter and

John here, Jesus always captured the attention of the individual that He wanted to heal, directing him to focus his gaze upon the Savior.

Why Look?

The reason for Peter's command was to arouse a sense of expectation, to quicken the lame man's faith. This man expected to receive something (probably money) from Peter and John. His faith was quickened by the command of Peter, "Look at us." There are people who go to church for years, yet whose lives show no evidence that God is at work. This is largely because they have never paid attention to Christ's command, *Look at me.* This is why Jesus always said to the people of His day, *He who has ears, let him hear.*

The minute Peter had the lame man's attention, he did two things that were most interesting. First, he admitted that he was bankrupt. "Silver and gold have I none," he said. "I know that's what you are looking for, but I can't help you there." And then he demonstrated his amazing adequacy in the spiritual realm. *In the name of Jesus of Nazareth, walk.* And in that electric moment, as this man was looking at Peter and John and heard these words—at the mention of the name of Jesus—strength came flowing into his ankles, and Peter, sensing it, took him by the right hand and lifted him up. The man stood up and began to shout and leap around, trying out this new-found strength in his legs which he had never known, because he had been lame from birth. No wonder it had such an amazing effect upon the people:

> And all the people saw him walking and praising God, and recognized him as the one who sat for alms at the Beautiful Gate of the temple; and they were filled with wonder and amazement at what had happened to him (Acts 3:9,10).

The people were immediately convinced, beyond a shadow of a doubt, that God was at work. They heard and saw this healing, and they noted that it was done in the name of Jesus, that name which signifies all that Jesus Christ is.

No Magic

To other people, everything that you are to them is evoked by your name. Whatever they see in you is what your name means to them. When you sign your name on a check, that check is good up to the value of what you have in the bank. It releases that amount to the person to whom the check is addressed. The name of Jesus here was not a magic formula that Peter used to produce a miracle. Rather, Peter was saying, "This is the power on whom I am depending. I'm not reckoning on silver and gold. In fact, that is not really what you need." Undoubtedly this beggar did have a material need—food and clothing and other things—but that is not what Peter offered him, because he did not have it. He offered him instead the authority and power and resources of the name of Jesus. All that Jesus was, was working through Peter at that time.

The Ground for Witness

That is exactly what the church is called to do; we are to declare our bankruptcy in the realm of the material. The church is not called to meet the material needs of the world. Now of course it is not wrong to give money. The parable of the good Samaritan keeps us in balance here. But the basic call of the church is to release the life of God, to declare the power of God, and to make available to men in the name of Jesus the things that only God can do. That is what these people saw, and they were convinced that God was at work.

This is the basic pattern for witness. If you want to be an effective witness for Jesus you don't just learn a set of facts about Christianity and go out and peddle these as though you were selling magazines and needed so many subscriptions to the Christian faith. Witness always follows this pattern: first God works. God does something. God changes a life—something that only God can do. Man cannot do it at all. And then man explains what God did. The person to whom it happened says what happened to him. That is what witness is. As a result of this cycle God works again, and another ground of witness—and an explanation—is given. This has been the pattern of witness down through the ages of Christianity.

Effective witness does not begin with an explanation. The normal pattern is to let God do something, and then as people see what God has done they ask you what happened. That is why Peter says, "Always be prepared to make a defence to anyone who calls you to account for the hope that is in you, yet do it with gentleness and reverence" (1 Pet. 3:15). That is what witnessing is.

Let's look more closely now at the event—and the subject—of healing. On the basis of this remarkable miracle in the Book of Acts many people say, "This is what ought to be occurring in the church all the time. People ought to be healed like this every day. Someone should walk up to them and say, 'In the name of Jesus of Nazareth rise and walk.'" Some people say that it is actually wrong for a Christian to be sick, that Jesus died not only for our sins but also for our sicknesses, and that "with his stripes we are healed" (Isa. 53:5). They claim that Christians who rely on doctors or medicines are revealing a terrible lack of faith, for God has provided physical healing just as much as He has provided redemption.

The idea that Jesus bore our sicknesses by His stripes (in that He was beaten for us) is a very popular concept, and it is the basis for the activity of many faith healers, who tell people that God expects them to be well, and that it is only their lack of faith that keeps them from being well. In these meetings people are exhorted to come up and let someone pray for them so that they may be healed immediately. Is this what this account suggests to us?

Signs of an Apostle

To answer this question, we need to look at the two classes of Scripture passages which deal with the subject of healing. By doing so we will find the two purposes for healing set forth in

Scripture. First, certain passages clearly indicate that healing miracles were intended to be authentications of the message of the gospel, and that the healers were really genuine messengers of God. God spoke through them. A passage which is often used as evidence of this purpose in healing is found in Mark, in which Jesus is meeting with His disciples after the resurrection. He tells them,

> Go into all the world and preach the gospel to the whole creation. He who believes and is baptized will be saved; but he who does not believe will be condemned (Mark 16:15,16).

And then He says,

> And these signs will accompany those who believe: in my name they will cast out demons; they will speak in new tongues; they will pick up serpents, and if they drink any deadly thing it will not hurt them; they will lay their hands on the sick, and they will recover (Mark 16:17,18).

Many movements have been based on the idea that this is the prerogative of every believer. But we need to notice in this passage from Mark's highly condensed account that Jesus *first* said to *all* of His disciples, "Go and preach the gospel to every creature," and then He added, "*He* [singular] who believes the gospel and is baptized will be saved; but *he* [singular] who does not believe will be condemned." Then Jesus changed back to the plural: "And these signs will accompany *those* who believe." By this He meant those disciples to whom He was talking, those whom He had just rebuked for their unbelief. Jesus had just finished scolding them because they would not believe that He was risen from the dead, so He added, "And these signs will accompany those [among you] who believe." Believe what? Believe in Christ's resurrection—that Jesus was really alive and that they had seen Him. Then Mark says this about the disciples:

> And *they* went forth and preached everywhere, while the Lord worked with them and confirmed the message by the signs that attended it (Mark 16:20).

These are what Paul calls "the signs of an apostle"—"signs and wonders and mighty works" (2 Cor. 12:12). So this promise was given to the disciples simply as an *authentication of their initial ministry*. It is not to be claimed by anyone and everyone who believes the gospel. This temporary authentication is confirmed by the writer to the Hebrews, who says that the Lord first preached the gospel:

> And it was attested to us *by those who heard him*, while God also bore witness by signs and wonders and various miracles. . . (Heb. 2:3,4).

There is another group of Scripture passages that indicates that God by His grace does heal in any age and at any time, though only according to His divine purpose. God is a gracious Father, and certain verses suggest that we have every right to ask Him to heal us physically, and that He will often choose to do so. In James we are told that if anyone is sick he is to call the elders together and let them pray. God will hear the prayer of faith and raise the sick. It also says, "Confess your sins to one another, and pray for one another, that you may be healed" (Jas. 5:16). But God does not categorically promise to heal. In numerous cases in Scripture God definitely chose *not* to heal, even among those who were strong in faith. When Paul wrote to the Philippians he referred to his dear friend and theirs, Epaphroditus. They had heard that he had been sick, and Paul said,

> Indeed he was ill, near to death. But God had mercy on him, and not only on him but on me also, lest I should have sorrow upon sorrow (Phil. 2:27).

Here is a clear instance when the Apostle himself, mighty man of God that he was, could not heal a sick friend. But God nevertheless spared Epaphroditus and restored him.

Inner Miracles

Someone has well said that every miracle is a parable. It is designed not only to demonstrate the power of God—a power that can literally heal instantaneously and completely—but it is also designed to illustrate people's need in symbolic form, and what happens in their inner life. What happens to your body is not nearly as important as what happens inside you. Moment by moment your body is getting older and grayer and stiffer and more difficult to maneuver and manipulate. But what is happening inside? That is the important thing. Paul says, "The outward man perishes, but the inward man is being renewed day by day." These outward miracles are pictures of what happens in the inward life; inside you can be crippled, blinded, or oppressed. All of these physical afflictions have spiritual counterparts.

This miracle occurred at the beginning of the age as a parable, to teach us what the age is like. This lame man is a picture of the world, lying at the door of God, asking for help. Here is a sick, lame, crippled society, unable to be the kind of men and women God wants them to be, and looking in vain to the church, to the door of God, for help. They do not know what to ask for; neither did the lame man. They ask largely for material help. But what is needed is what Peter and John gave—not silver and gold, but the name of Jesus, the power of a new life, the impartation of a new strength that results in a lame man becoming whole.

When I was at a theological seminary in Denver I met a boy who told me that he was the ping-pong champion of Colorado. He lived for ping-pong. He thought it was tremendous. Ping-pong was his whole life. But after he became champion he said it all turned to dust and ashes in his mouth. He discovered that man is made for bigger things than ping-pong. He found Jesus Christ, and in finding Him he was made whole, and ping-pong meant nothing to him anymore. This incident may sound humorous, but that is the lesson of this miracle. God is offering to heal men and women and make them whole, mature, and grown up—not only physically, but also spiritually. As the healing hand of Jesus Christ is laid again and again on our hearts and our lives we are being made whole, as God intended men and women to be. This is the great message which we need to declare today: *In the name of Jesus Christ of Nazareth, rise up and walk, and be what God wants you to be.*

Chapter Seven

The Only Solution

Acts 3:11-26

As Peter took the lame beggar by the hand and lifted him up, the man's ankles and bones received strength and he began to leap and shout and walk around the temple courts, praising God. Now Luke continues the account with a report of what immediately followed this amazing incident:

> While he clung to Peter and John, all the people ran together to them in the portico called Solomon's, astounded. And when Peter saw it he addressed the people, "Men of Israel, why do you wonder at this, or why do you stare at us, as though by our own power or piety we had made him walk?" (Acts 3:11,12).

Picture the scene in your imagination. This healed cripple, in his unbounded joy, is holding on to Peter and John with both arms. They try to get away, but he won't let them go. In the Greek it means that he clung to them with great strength. The people around, seeing this commotion, rush over to Solomon's porch in the temple and recognize the man who had formerly sat begging at the Beautiful Gate. Then they stare in silent astonishment at what they see. Peter, looking at their faces, notices their astonishment—the fact that they were stunned by what had happened. He also senses a developing reverence for himself and John—a misguided hero worship. This told him that these people, like many today, really did not believe in a God who could act in history.

Even though they had previously seen Jesus perform many miracles like this one, they were absolutely astonished at this healing. Peter also noticed that the people were ready to substitute a false explanation. They started attributing the healing to some kind of magical power on the part of Peter and John. This provides the background for Peter's address, in which he explains what happened.

The key to this message is in his opening words, "Men of Israel." There is a very definite Hebraic cast to what Peter says now, because he recognizes that the people to whom he is speaking are all Israelites. In his opening question the word *you* should be underscored: "Men of Israel, why do *you* wonder at this?" "You should know better. You ought to know that God is this kind of God. He has acted many times in your history in this way." I don't think we can fully understand this passage unless we see that Peter has the background of these people well in mind, and that he understands that they know the Scriptures and ought to have anticipated something like this.

Begin with the Facts

The message that Peter gives falls very easily into three divisions, and in each of these divisions Peter says a most startling thing. In the first section he presents a series of facts which could hardly fail to arouse the people's guilt. Psychologists tell us today that the worst thing you can do in trying to help someone is to arouse a sense of guilt—that if you make someone feel guilty you shut the door to any real help to him. But in this message Peter moves without hesitation to a recital of facts that arouses the guilt of these people:

> The God of Abraham and of Isaac and of Jacob, the God of our fathers, glorified his servant Jesus, whom you delivered up and denied in the presence of Pilate, when he had decided to release him. But you denied the Holy and Righteous One, and asked for a murderer to be granted to you, and killed the Author of life, whom God raised from the dead. To this we are witnesses (Acts 3:13-15).

Christianity always rests upon facts, and facts are what Peter puts before these people—real events in which these very listeners had been deeply and inextricably involved. Notice the contrast which Peter draws between the acts of God and the acts of men. He says that God, the God of your fathers, the God whom you have worshipped—this God glorified His servant Jesus, but you delivered Him up to be crucified. And furthermore, the man to whom you delivered Him, Pilate, was a pagan, a Gentile ruler who did not have the background of theology and the understanding of God's activity that you have, and yet he was convinced of Christ's innocence and tried to release Him. But you—you denied Him. And third, the One you denied was the Holy and Righteous One. These are terms which these Hebrews would have understood, because they are Old Testament names applied to Messiah; they are names that recognize His deity—that the One who was coming would be God Himself.

And, says Peter, you not only denied the Holy and Righteous One when He came, but you also asked for a murderer, Barabbas, to be granted to you. In other words, you denied the Giver of life and asked instead that a taker of life be delivered up to you. Furthermore, Peter continues, you killed the Author of life—a word that is better translated the Pioneer of life, the first One who had life. This refers to Jesus as the first human being ever to be resurrected—not just restored to physical life but raised to a higher level. Though you killed Him, Peter says, God answered you by raising Him from the dead.

All these facts, Peter continues, were attested to by witnesses: "We are witnesses of this." This is another striking confirmation that the Christian faith is not a religion of dreamy ideas or sentimental hopes, but that it rests on facts that can be attested to by witnesses, as in a court of law. The people who were listening to Peter could not deny that these things had happened, and as a result (as on the Day of Pentecost) they were cut to the heart by the conviction of their guilt. To me the joy of Christianity is the way in which God's Word of truth cuts right through all the illusion, fantasy, and dream worlds that we build around ourselves—right through to reality. The conventional idea that Jesus and His apostles were misty-eyed dreamers who went around talking about beautiful worlds and idyllic ideas is exploded when you start reading the Scriptures. There you discover that it is Jesus and His apostles who are the hard-nosed realists, the ones who are always injecting hard truths into a world ruled by illusion.

The Forces of Guilt

Why did Peter start right out by making these people feel such a terrible load of guilt? Psychologists rightly tell us that guilt is a destructive force in human lives. We cannot live with guilt. Yet the fundamental characteristic of fallen man is that he feels guilty. There is not a person in the world who does not experience guilt. And the disturbing, unhappy feeling of guilt quickly produces other emotions, like fear. Remember when you were little and you did things that displeased your parents, and then you felt guilty? Your immediate reaction was to hide, because you were afraid. Fear is an unpleasant companion to live with. It motivates a person to run and hide, to escape in some form, or else it makes him hostile, resentful, and bitter. Fear that leads to escape soon becomes despair; life soon loses all its color and meaning. Fear that moves to hostility—a feeling of resentment or bitterness—eventually results in violence. And violence destroys the humanity of an individual.

So why would Peter want to awaken this negative force of guilt in the hearts of his hearers? The answer is that before the guilt and fear which is awakened by these words can lead to either escape or hostility, Peter moves to his next point—God's answer to the problem of human guilt. Peter beautifully describes a faith which lays hold of the grace of God:

And his name, by faith in his name, has made this man strong whom you see and know; and the faith which is through Jesus has given the man this perfect health in the presence of you all (Acts 3:16).

Here is a lame man who is part of this guilty nation. Although he was handicapped and incapacitated in himself, he was also part of the nation which had rejected its Messiah and had cried out "Crucify him! Crucify him!" when Pilate had wanted to let Jesus go. The lame man was just as guilty as anyone else in the crowd, yet here he stands in perfect health, restored whole by God's power. The basis of his acceptance before God, says Peter, the only thing that made God do this wonderful thing in his life, was simply his faith in the name of Jesus. In this restoration of physical health God demonstrated how He reacts to human guilt. He reacts in love and grace, on the basis of faith in the name of Jesus. "Don't look at us," says Peter; "We didn't do it. When we spoke the name of Jesus, this man believed in the power and authority of that name. And immediately the strength that his limbs lacked came flowing into his body."

Out of Ignorance

With exhibit "A" standing right before the eyes of his hearers, Peter now goes on to declare to them what the result can be in their own lives:

> And now, brethren, I know that you acted in ignorance, as did also your rulers. But what God foretold by the mouth of all the prophets, that his Christ should suffer, he thus fulfilled. Repent therefore, and turn again, that your sins may be blotted out, that times of refreshing may come from the presence of the Lord, and that he may send the Christ appointed for you, Jesus, whom heaven must receive until the time for establishing all that God spoke by the mouth of his holy prophets from of old (Acts 3:17-21).

Here Peter declares that God's answer to man's condemnation of His Son and rejection of the Lord of life is a forgiveness and restoration which take into account man's ignorant blindness. God sees what you did, says Peter, not as the deliberate act of a perverted and twisted will trying to strike back against God, but as the blundering act of an ignorant mind that doesn't realize what it is doing.

In these words there is perhaps an echo in Peter's memory of the words which Peter heard Jesus Himself speak on the Cross when he prayed, "Father, forgive them, for they know not what they do." Here, and perhaps nowhere else as clearly, we see how God sees man. He sees him as ignorant, blind, and stupid, blundering along in his darkness, not knowing what he is doing. In trying to run our world today it is becoming very clear that we don't know what we are doing. So often people say, "Oh, I had no idea what I was doing! I was just trying to do the right thing, but I've just loused everything up!" And that is exactly what God expects of us, what He has been trying to tell us all along. It is only man's pride that makes him boast about all his achievements while ignoring his weakness and folly. Not only in matters of politics and economics is this true, but it is especially evident in the realm of ecology, where we have poisoned our lakes and loaded our air so heavily with pollutants that we cannot see the mountains a few miles away.

Refreshment and Restoration

Peter then goes on to announce what God's purpose is. "Repent therefore, and turn again, unto the blotting out of your sins, and two great things will happen: times of refreshing will come from the face of the Father, and He will ultimately send Jesus Christ to you to restore all the things which were spoken of by the prophets." Peter, looking forward through the whole age, says, "Here are the principles by which God is going to operate: wherever there is a turning back to Him, there will be an immediate dealing with the problem of guilt. God blots out sins."

For some reason there is nothing harder for people to do than to believe God. Countless Christians are still trying to work out some standing or merit before God, to do something to make themselves acceptable to Him. But Peter says that God arouses guilt only because He has the *solution* to it, the blotting out of sins in the name of Jesus.

When that happens, Peter says, there will come times of refreshing—periods in human history which will be characterized by relative peace, prosperity, order, and joy. After the spiritual awakening through the Wesleys, England was saved from the disaster of revolution which the French had just gone through. The country was turned around and, although there were still many problems, England experienced joy and contentment. The Protestant reformation in Germany, under Martin Luther, was also such a time.

Furthermore, says Peter, it will result ultimately in the return of Jesus Christ. This confirms what I had long suspected from the Scriptures: that when Jesus Christ returns He will not come back at a low ebb of faith, but rather at the height of an awakening, when God's people have returned to Him and there is a release of the fullness of the power of the Spirit. The world around will be barren and disconsolate, but there will be a time of life and vitality on the part of the people of God.

The Personal Question

Now Peter closes with this appeal to act:

Moses said, "The Lord God will raise up for you a prophet from your brethren, as he raised me up. You shall listen to him in whatever he tells you. And it shall be that every soul that does not listen to the prophet shall be destroyed from the people." And all the prophets who have spoken, from Samuel and those who came afterwards, also proclaimed these days. You are the sons of the prophets and of the covenant which God gave to your fathers, saying to Abraham, "And in your posterity shall all the families of the earth be blessed." God, having raised up his servant, sent him to you first, to bless you in turning every one of you from your wickedness (Acts 3:22-26).

Paul tells us that historically the gospel was to go first to the Jew and then to the Gentile, and that is the program which is followed in the Book of Acts. Soon God will turn to the Gentile world, for in Christ there is neither Jew nor Gentile. But now Peter argues, "Look, you are Jews. You know the prophets; you have been reading them. And your own Scriptures urge you to believe in Jesus." Then Peter drives home the point with a personal emphasis: "God has sent Him to *you,* to turn *you* from your wickedness." Perhaps Peter learned his Old Testament application to the Christian life during those 40 days after the resurrection, when Jesus opened the disciples' minds to understand the Scriptures: "Beginning with Moses and all the prophets, he interpreted to them in all the scriptures the things concerning himself" (Luke 24:27). Peter is saying, "Each man of you has to settle this for himself. Will *you* allow God to turn *you* from your wickedness? Will you begin at the place where God begins, right at your own heart, with your own problem of guilt, with your own lack of acceptance before God? Will you deal with that before Jesus Christ, and will you in the name of Jesus believe that God loves you and receives you and makes you His own, and that you are privileged to live as His child, His son, right now?" That is all that Peter can do; the rest is up to those who hear. Will they respond? It is their choice.

Chapter Eight

The Threat of the Resurrection

Acts 4:1-12

As Peter and John stood on the steps of the temple, speaking with mighty power to the assembled crowd, there was a sudden, violent interruption:

> And as they were speaking to the people, the priests and the captain of the temple and the Sadducees came upon them, annoyed because they were teaching the people and proclaiming in Jesus the resurrection from the dead. And they arrested them and put them in custody until the morrow, for it was already evening. But many of those who heard the word believed; and the number of the men came to about five thousand (Acts 4:1-4).

There was a tremendous popular response to Peter's message that day—we are told that five thousand men believed (women and children weren't counted in those days!). But suddenly there was this display of authoritative, iron-fisted power as the temple guards elbowed their way through the crowd, surrounded Peter and John, arrested them, dragged them off, and put them in jail until the next day.

The most remarkable thing about this arrest is the reason. These apostles were not proclaiming the overthrow of the Roman government. If they had been, we might have expected such a reaction from the authorities. Nor were they protesting against some of the social evils of the day. Peter raised not a word of protest against the widespread practice of slavery throughout the empire, even though half the people in the Roman Empire were slaves. Nor did he say anything about the burdens of excessive taxation which the Romans had lowered on these people. No, the message which the authorities regarded as too radical to tolerate was the simple proclamation of Jesus and His resurrection from the dead. For this message Peter and John were thrown into jail before they could even finish their speech. Yet because of this proclamation five thousand men in that great crowd in Jerusalem became believers in Jesus Christ.

Cause for Alarm

Do you think this kind of arrest could take place today? Would today's authorities oppose a message like this? Well, the clear answer of current history is that they would, and they do. There are several large governments on earth today that are so fearful of the message of Jesus that they use every weapon at their command to keep this radical message from penetrating to their people. Even in our own country this message is sometimes opposed. In a recent awakening in our high schools scores of students came to know Jesus Christ. Yet that awakening, that power that turned these kids from drugs and futility, has aroused suspicion in many people. Many people would gladly suppress and stifle this whole affair.

What were the elements of Peter's proclamation that were so disturbing to the authorities? What offensive thing did these apostles say when they proclaimed in Jesus the resurrection from the dead? First, of course, they proclaimed the great and exciting fact that Jesus Christ Himself had risen from the dead only seven weeks before the event of Pentecost took place, and that they, along with over a hundred other disciples, were witnesses to this fact. So powerful was their testimony that not a single voice was raised to challenge it. Instead, five thousand people became convinced of its truth, just as three thousand people had been convinced a few days earlier, on the Day of Pentecost.

The disciples also preached that Jesus had extended the promise of the resurrection to others as well; He had said, "I am the resurrection and the life; he who believes in me, though he die, yet shall he live" (John 11:25). Jesus also said, "Because I live, you shall live also." Out of the open tomb of Jesus has arisen a radiant, flaming hope that has gripped and held the hearts of millions of believers in the face of persecution and death. Even in the midst of the bleak helplessness of watching a loved one die, faith in the resurrection of the dead in Jesus can bring peace—yes, even joy—to an anguished heart.

Death Is Death

But if this is all that the apostles had had to say, they would not have created quite the stir that they did. This crowd was made up mostly of Jews, and they knew already from the Old Testament Scriptures that there was hope beyond the grave. It was the third dramatic element that Peter proclaimed on this day that made all the difference in the world. He undoubtedly explained to these people that physical death is strangely linked with the death that is at work in our inner lives right now, that death is all one thing. We experience that inner death a thousand ways, sometimes as loneliness, sometimes as bitterness, sometimes as emptiness and despair, sometimes as depression of spirit. Sometimes it is boredom, sometimes hate; sometimes it is malice and resentment and violence. Whatever it may be, it is not what God intended for man; it is an enemy that haunts him every moment.

The glorious proclamation of the truth as it is in Jesus is that Jesus Christ did something about this form of death as well; He overcame it by His resurrection. As a result restlessness is replaced by peace, guilt by acceptance, lust by love, and weakness by power. There is joy for mourning, beauty for ashes, hope for despair, and courage for cowardice. So desperate were these people, so tired of emptiness and of sin, that five thousand hearts leaped to believe and turn to Christ, to begin a new life in Him.

Wouldn't you think that the authorities would be pleased, that the rulers of the city would be happy that men and women were finding the answer to their lifelong search? Why, then, were they so annoyed with this event? Well, it's clear that they sensed a threat; they felt it in their bones. They stopped the whole show until they could put their finger on just what it was that bothered them, as we read in this next section:

> On the morrow their rulers and elders and scribes were gathered together in Jerusalem, with Annas the high priest and Caiaphas and John and Alexander, and all who were of the high-priestly family. And when they had set them in the midst, they inquired, "By what power or by what name did you do this?" Then Peter, filled with the Holy Spirit, said to them, "Rulers of the people and elders, if we are being examined today concerning a good deed done to a cripple, by what means this man has been healed, be it known to you all, and to all the people of Israel, that by the name of Jesus Christ of Nazareth, whom you crucified, whom God raised from the dead, by him this man is standing before you well. This is the stone which was rejected by you builders, but which has become the head of the corner. And there is salvation in no one else, for there is no other name under heaven given among men by which we must be saved" (Acts 4:5-12).

You can see how seriously the authorities took all this by Luke's careful listing of those who were present. There was Annas, who was the honorary high priest, the father of Caiaphas. Then there was Caiaphas, who was the official high priest, and with them were gathered two of his brothers, John and Alexander. We know from secular history that this family of the high priest constituted a ruling class in Jerusalem, controlling the vast wealth of the temple and certain profitable monopolies connected with the sacrifice. Here was the class that was in power and authority, with great political and economical vested interests throughout the city. They were greatly disturbed, for they sensed a threat to their power. They were so disturbed, in fact, that without realizing what they were doing they gave Peter an open door for testimony.

Send Up the Cornerstone!

The authorities said to Peter, "Tell us, by what power or what name have you done this thing?" This was just what Peter was waiting for. With delight he tells them, "By the name of the man whom you crucified, whom God raised from the dead." What a contrast Peter presents with the disciple who cringed before a maid in the high priest's courtyard a few weeks earlier! On that occasion Peter denied that he knew Jesus three times before the cock crowed. But what a difference now. The bold Apostle is filled with the Holy Spirit as the life of Jesus is being imparted to him. With the boldness of a lion Peter says,

By the name of Jesus Christ of Nazareth, whom you crucified, whom God raised from the dead, by him this man is standing before you well (Acts 4:10).

The former lame man was right there with the authorities, standing as undeniable evidence of the power and authority of the name of Jesus Christ. Then, to further drive the point home, Peter quotes from Psalm 118:22:

This is the stone which was rejected by you builders, but which has become the head of the corner (Acts 4:11).

What Peter and the Psalm are referring to is the occasion of the building of Solomon's temple. The Bible tells us that when Solomon built his temple on the place where the Dome of the Rock now stands in Jerusalem, there was no sound of hammer or saws and no pounding of any kind. The temple was erected in silence. The rocks that formed the temple were taken from a quarry underneath where the temple stands. If you go to Jerusalem, you can go down to what they call Solomon's quarries and see that it is solid rock. And from that rock the temple was built. It was built to such exacting blueprint dimensions that each rock was shaped perfectly before it ever left the quarry, so that when it reached the temple it could be put in place without any hammering or pounding of any kind.

According to Jewish tradition, during the building of the temple a great rock was quarried and shaped by the master mason, but when the builders received it they could find no place to put it. It didn't seem to match any of the blueprints they were working from, so they placed it to one side. After awhile, because the rock seemed to be in the way, someone pushed it over the edge of a bank and it rolled down into the Kidron Valley and was lost in the bushes. But when the time came to hoist the cornerstone, the great square rock that held everything else in place, no one could seem to find it. The masons sent word that the cornerstone had already been delivered some time earlier, so the on-site builders looked around some more for it, but still no one could seem to find it. Then someone remembered the huge "extra" rock that had been pushed over the edge. Down they went to the valley, where they found it lying in the bushes. With great effort the builders returned the rejected stone to the temple site and hoisted it into place, where it fit perfectly as the cornerstone of the temple.

That's what Peter meant when he quoted this Psalm. God had planned that Jesus of Nazareth would be the cornerstone of His government on earth, the Rock upon which all human government would rest and from which it would take all its authority. But the builders of the various nations rejected the cornerstone. So Peter thundered the accusation, "You rejected Him when He came! You had the chance to build a government of Jerusalem on the Rock which God ordained, but you rejected the Rock by crucifying God's Son! But God nevertheless raised Him from the dead and made Him the Head of the corner." Then Peter added these amazing words:

And there is salvation in no one else, for there is no other name under heaven given among men by which we must be saved (Acts 4:12).

This is a startling declaration. It says that no one but Jesus can qualify as the cornerstone. There is only One Person who is adequately equipped to be the foundation of all human government, the basis of all human authority.

Truth with Power

Christians are often accused of being bigoted and intolerant of other faiths. In one sense this accusation is perfectly true. We *are* intolerant of other faiths in the final analysis. But this doesn't mean that Christians don't recognize certain truths in other religions. Some great religious leaders have uttered certain fine moral teachings and helpful precepts. But there is one thing they have never done: though they can tell us what is right to do, they can never enable us to actually do it. That is the crucial difference between Jesus of Nazareth and any other name that can be named in this world. That is why we can never consent to putting any other name on an equal with Jesus of Nazareth. No other person has solved the problem of death. No other person has broken through this ghastly terror that hangs over the human race except Jesus of Nazareth.

Most of us don't need someone to tell us what to do; we already know what we should be doing. As Mark Twain said, "I don't need anyone to tell me what to do. I'm not doing half of what I know to do, now." What we need is someone who will make us *want* to do what we ought to do—to give us a new heart, a new outlook, a new ability, a new capacity, a new life. That is what Jesus of Nazareth does again and again—and that is political heresy. Whenever this miracle takes place it threatens all oppression and tyranny wherever it may prevail in the world.

The life of Jesus Christ is never against government as such, but it is against *oppressive* government. His life is the foundation of Christian liberties everywhere. There has never been a force more powerful to assure liberation of men and women from oppression than the dramatic power of Christ's resurrection. That is why this event is hated by the totalitarian forces of our day, whoever they may be. But the glorious fact is that this event is what God is going to build His kingdom on. Christ has become the Head of the corner. Behind the scenes of tyranny and heartbreak and tears and anguish all around us God is working out His purposes. He is building a new humanity, inviting men and women everywhere to share in the risen life of Jesus Christ, and to experience *now* the glory of a life of peace and joy and rest.

Chapter Nine

When Obedience is Wrong

Acts 4:13-31

The leaders of the powerful ruling class of Jerusalem, confronted with the unassailable fact of a lame man healed, were also being confronted with a far more uncomfortable fact—that Jesus of Nazareth, whom they thought they were rid of, was somehow still alive. Their uneasiness and uncertainty was obvious:

> Now when they saw the boldness of Peter and John, and perceived that they were uneducated, common men, they wondered; and they recognized that they had been with Jesus. But, seeing the man that had been healed standing beside them, they had nothing to say in opposition. But when they had commanded them to go aside out of the council, they conferred with one another, saying, "What shall we do with these men? For that a notable sign has been performed through them is manifest to all the inhabitants of Jerusalem, and we cannot deny it" (Acts 4:13-16).

This is a remarkable picture of the perversity of human hearts. Surely these men—high priests and rulers of the city—would have prided themselves on being logical, reasonable, consistent men who acted on the basis of facts. We always think of ourselves this way. But this account makes very clear that they were utterly self-deceived. Although they thought they were acting from a rational position, they were actually operating contrary to reason.

Luke points out that these men first noted an unexpected

boldness in Peter and John, a note of authority in their voice, a certain poise that these rulers were not used to seeing in uneducated men. They had expected to find this kind of authority only in educated men, but they could see from the dress of the apostles that these were untrained, common men. In the language of the New English Bible, the apostles were "untrained laymen," and these Jewish rulers were at a loss to understand this. How could uneducated, common men have such poise and confidence? The conclusion they came to is most remarkable: these men must have been with Jesus!

These Jewish rulers had had difficulty with Jesus; nothing they had said or done to Him ever seemed to trouble Him. Now here were men who were reflecting the same spirit. The high priest and the rest of the rulers had apparently become aware of the fact that anyone who had anything to do with Jesus for very long began to act differently, showing an obvious confidence, an air of boldness and quiet authority. So these Jewish rulers were forced to conclude that these men had been with Jesus.

The second thing they noticed was the continuous evidence of the man made whole. It was evident that no crime had been committed; it is no crime to heal a sick man! A good deed had been done, and they could hardly deny it. They were therefore at a loss to know what to do with these men, what charge they could level against them.

An Illegal Act

The third point Luke records is that the rulers admitted to themselves (after the apostles had been sent out) that the nature of this act of healing was a sign. These men were acquainted with the meaning and value of signs. They were the rulers of a nation which had a unique relationship to God, a relationship which, throughout the course of Israel's history, had been characterized by the giving of signs. God had frequently manifested His presence in an unmistakable manner and confirmed His message by accompanying signs. Now the reasonable, logical, sensible reaction to this kind of evidence would be to acknowledge that the sign came from God and to support these men in their cause. But notice their conclusion:

> "But in order that it may spread no further among the people, let us warn them to speak no more to anyone in this name." So they called them and charged them not to speak or teach at all in the name of Jesus (Acts 4:17,18).

That was exactly contrary to the evidence they had received!

> But Peter and John answered them, "Whether it is right in the sight of God to listen to you rather than to God, you must judge; for we cannot but speak of what we have seen and heard." And when they had further threatened them, they let them go, finding no way to punish them, because of the people; for all men praised God for what had happened. For the man on whom this sign of healing was performed was more than forty years old (Acts 4:19-22).

The inconsistency of these rulers led to what was basically an illegal act. They were the representatives of God to the nation of Israel, and as such they were ostensibly committed to doing the will and purpose of God. Yet here, in spite of the evidence they had received of what God wanted done, they directly opposed the will and word of God and forbade these apostles to speak in the name of Jesus. The disciples very wisely and courteously declined to obey this command. They pointed out that they had no choice; they could not but "speak the things they had seen and heard." The message they declared was so challenging, so transforming in its implications—both to the nation and to the world—that they could not be silent and still be true to their relationship to God. They therefore respectfully declined to obey what these rulers commanded. The priests could only bluster and threaten the apostles because they feared the people, for the apostles had the support of the populace.

Whom to Obey?

At this point the whole question of civil disobedience comes into view. Here is a clear case of it. These apostles were forbidden by the properly constituted authorities (the establishment, we would call them), to preach in the name of Jesus. The apostles told the rulers to their faces that they would not obey their order. This incident has been used many times since then, and especially in our own day, to justify such activities as racial strife, draft evasion, violent demonstration, boycotts, strikes, and so forth. We cannot read this account without the question being raised, and quite properly: Is it right for a Christian to disobey a law because of a conscientious scruple? It is clear from this account that there are times when it is necessary and right to disobey properly constituted authority. The establishment can be wrong as well as right.

But it is also important to notice from this account that civil disobedience occurs here *only* because the conscience of these men rested directly on a *clear and unmistakable precept of God* which contravened the human law. The issue is so clear here that Peter actually calls on the rulers to be the judges as to what the apostles should do. He says, "Whether it is right in the sight of God to listen to you rather than to God, you must judge." You are religious men, he implies; you know which is the higher authority. Which should we obey, God or you? God or man? The matter was so clear that the only thing the authorities *could* say was, "Obey God rather than us." Yet instead they threatened and blustered, hoping to maintain control by the threat of force. They feared the people, who were convinced that this was indeed a remarkable sign from God.

Here, then, are the Biblical grounds for civil disobedience. The Scriptures state very clearly that governments are given by God. The Apostle Paul says that governing authorities are the servants of God (Rom. 13:1-7). It is important to note that when Paul wrote these words the supreme governing authority was none other than Nero—a wicked, vile, godless man, one of the worst emperors the Romans ever had. Yet Paul could write that the governing authorities were the servants of God, and that those who resist them are resisting what God has ordained. Paul acknowledges that governments have certain powers, derived not from the people but from God: the power to tax, the power to keep law and order, and the power to punish evildoing, even to the point of death. We must conclude, then, that the human conscience operating alone, unsupported by a word of revelation from God, does not supply the basis for disobeying the law. The law of man, even bad law, is superior to conscience unless that conscience rests upon a direct precept of God.

Conscience is not intended to tell us right from wrong. Conscience can be wrong as well as right. In fact, apart from the help of revealed truth, our conscience would only lead us all astray. Let me share a quotation from H. C. Trumbull, a very clear-thinking writer:

> Conscience is not given to a man to instruct him in the right, but to prompt him to choose the right instead of the wrong when he is instructed as to what is right. It tells a man that he ought to do right, but does not tell him what is right. And if a man has made up his mind that a certain wrong course is the right one, the more he follows his conscience the more helpless he is as a wrongdoer. One is pretty far gone in an evil way when he serves the devil conscientiously.

It is only when there is a clear-cut case of conflict between the word and will of God and the word and will of man (as in this case) that conscience is superior to law.

Everything's Under Control

Notice where the apostles go for redress and support:

> When they were released they went to their friends and reported what the chief priests and the elders had said to them. And when they heard it, they lifted their voices together to God and said, "Sovereign Lord, who didst make the heaven and the earth and the sea and everything in them, who by the mouth of our father David, thy servant, didst say by the Holy Spirit, 'Why did the Gentiles rage, and the peoples imagine vain things? The kings of the earth set themselves in array, and the rulers were gathered together, against the Lord and against his Anointed'---for truly in this city there were gathered together against thy holy servant Jesus, whom thou didst

anoint, both Herod and Pontius Pilate, with the Gentiles and the peoples of Israel, to do whatever thy hand and thy plan had predestined to take place" (Acts 4:23-28).

These apostles did not go out to organize a revolutionary committee to overthrow the Sanhedrin. They did not even try to arouse a popular march or demonstration, even though the people were behind them. The apostles did not rely for even one minute upon political or popular pressure. Instead, they cast themselves wholly upon the sovereign power of God at work in history.

The apostles found encouragement in two things. First, they trusted in the sovereignty of God—His overruling control of human events. The very first word of their prayer, "Sovereign Lord," in Greek is the word from which we get our word "despot." "O Mighty Despot (Tyrant, Ruler over men), who didst make the heaven and the earth and the sea and everything in them." God holds the world in the palm of His hand and is intimately involved in every human event, and in that truth the apostles found great consolation. They openly recognized that God had even predicted the very opposition they faced. They had clearly been doing what Christians ought to do under pressure: they had gone to the Scriptures. There they had found these words:

> Why did the Gentiles rage, and the peoples imagine vain things? The kings of the earth set themselves in array, and the rulers were gathered together, against the Lord and against his Anointed (Acts 4:25,26).

When they read this in the second Psalm they said to themselves, "There, that's exactly what has happened. Herod and Pontius Pilate, with the others, the Gentiles and the peoples of Israel, have set themselves against the Lord Jesus. We saw it happen right in this very city. It's exactly what God said would happen." They found great encouragement in the fact that this event was not beyond divine control, that the opposition they were facing was anticipated. God has power to overrule in any situation, so the apostles didn't try to arouse a popular uprising, which would only create violence; instead, they relied on the God who works in

strange and unusual ways to change human events without violence.

To Carry Out His Plan

The apostles were also encouraged by what we might call the
mystery of history. You can see it in the last sentence here:
"Herod and Pontius Pilate, with the Gentiles and the peoples of
Israel [were gathered together] to do *whatever thy hand and thy
plan had predestined to take place"* (Acts 4:27,28). In other
words, the God of history uses His very enemies to accomplish
His purposes! God works through the free will of man. These
people had opposed the plan of God. They had tried to thwart
God's purposes. They had tried to derail His program. But God
operates in such a marvelous way that He was able to use even
this opposition to accomplish His will. That is the story of the
Cross and of the resurrection of Jesus.

The principle that these Christians reckoned upon is the most
powerful force known to man—a power which the church frequently ignores to its peril. A powerfully poetic expression of the
overruling power of God is found in the New English Bible's
rendition of Job 12:10-25:

> In God's hand are the souls of all that live, the spirits of all
> humankind. . . .
> Wisdom and might are his; with him are firmness and under-
> standing.
> If he pulls down, there is no rebuilding; if he imprisons, there
> is no release.
> If he holds up the waters, there is drought; if he lets them go,
> they turn the land upside down.
> Strength and success belong to him; deceived and deceiver are
> his to use.
> He makes counselors behave like idiots and drives judges mad.
> He looses the bonds imposed by kings and removes the girdle
> of office from their waist.
> He makes priests behave like idiots and overthrows men long
> in office.

Those who are trusted he strikes dumb; he takes away the
judgment of old men.
He heaps scorn on princes and abates the arrogance of
nobles. . . .
He leads peoples astray and destroys them: he lays them low,
and there they lie.
He takes away their wisdom from the rulers of the nations and
leaves them wandering in a pathless wilderness.
They grope in the darkness without light and are left to
wander like a drunkard.

The overruling power of God is the true strength of the church.
As the weapon of faith-prayer it is tremendous in its possibilities.

Shakedown

Resting upon this power, these disciples now make their request:

And now, Lord, look upon their threats, and grant to thy
servants to speak thy word with all boldness, while thou
stretchest out thy hand to heal, and signs and wonders are
performed through the name of thy holy servant Jesus (Acts
4:29,30).

What they are saying in essence is, "Do it again, Lord. Do it again.
Here we are in trouble and our lives are in danger; do it again!"
They are asking for more.

And when they had prayed, the place in which they were
gathered together was shaken; and they were all filled with the
Holy Spirit and spoke the word of God with boldness (Acts
4:31).

In answer to this prayer by the apostles God first shook the place
in which they were praying. This was God's symbolic answer to
the disciples' prayer. He was saying to them, in a figurative way,
that He would shake Jerusalem and the world by the message
these disciples were proclaiming. Less than 40 years after this
event the city of Jerusalem was surrounded by Roman armies and
the authority of the priests was broken in the city. Ultimately the

entire nation of Israel was shaken and its people dispersed throughout the nations of the world. For almost twenty centuries Jewish government was not permitted to come into power again. The principles of Christianity then penetrated and permeated all strata of Roman society, changing and transforming them completely.

Many young people today are troubled by power structures, by the establishments. They see the evils in them, and that they are not doing what they were set up to do. But it is clear from this account that there is a mighty force at work in society, a force upon which you can rely to enable you to do what these disciples did—to proclaim a message which is the most powerful revolutionary proclamation the world has ever seen; to speak the Word of God with boldness in the filling of the Holy Spirit. To do this is to shake society to its very core.

The factor which produces peace, order, prosperity, blessing, and happiness in a land is not the form of government which exists. The U.S. Constitution will not ultimately protect us or preserve justice. What will preserve justice? Righteousness! A people who are dedicated to the will and purpose of God and who recognize the life of God in their midst. That is what preserves a land: that is the only thing that ever has or ever will. The lack of righteousness has been the prime reason for the overturn of one civilization after another. Arnold Toynbee has counted some 26 great civilizations that have come and gone. They failed because they were not built upon righteousness.

The effect of the message of Jesus and the resurrection is to bring new life pouring from a living Christ into dying and dead people and institutions, changing them, awakening them, arousing them again to righteousness, to living in accordance with reality. The only hope of our own nation is the proclamation of this message in every possible way in the fulness of the power of the Holy Spirit. God has made provision that we might do as these disciples did. Being filled with the Holy Spirit, let us speak the word with all boldness and produce a profoundly unsettling effect upon all the structures of society.

Chapter Ten

Great Power, Great Grace, Great Fear

Acts 4:32-5:11

One of the most exciting events of our exciting times is the overwhelming evidence that the Spirit of God is moving to heal a sluggish and diseased church. No one can really comprehend the death and darkness that prevails in the church in many places today unless they contrast it with the vitality and excitement of the normal Christian life. In the fourth chapter of Acts we find a beautiful glimpse of life in the early church. After the dramatic events of the Day of Pentecost, the healing of the lame man, and the great response of the multitudes in Jerusalem, the church faced life in a world of darkness, despair, and death—and it met that death with an outflowing of the life of Jesus Christ. Genuine Christianity is described for us in this way:

> Now the company of those who believed were of one heart and soul, and no one said that any of the things which he possessed was his own, but they had everything in common (Acts 4:32).

Unfortunately, a counterfeit Christianity came along very soon in this early church, and evidences of it can be seen throughout the Book of Acts. Wherever the true church has gone, counterfeit Christianity has kept close company with it. Counterfeit Christianity can be recognized externally as a kind of religious club where people who are mostly of the same social level and who are bound together by a mutual interest in some religious project or program meet to advance that particular cause. In distinct contrast, true Christianity consists of individuals who share the same divine life, who are made up of all ages, backgrounds, classes, and levels of society, and who understand that they are brothers and sisters in one family. Out of that background of mutual love and fellowship they manifest the life of Jesus Christ.

Belonging to Each Other

That is what we have in this verse. The last word is the key: ". . . they had everything in *common*." They were of one heart. At the very deepest level of their lives they belonged to each other, and that is only possible by means of the Holy Spirit. They recognized that they belonged to each other, that they were of the same family and had a great deal in common.

Not only were they of one heart, compelled by the Holy Spirit to share the life of Jesus together, but they were also of one soul. Most of us read the words "they were of one heart and soul" as though it were simply a double way of saying a single thing. But the soul is different from the heart, or the spirit. The soul is the conscious part of life, and it consists of the mind and emotions and will. Whatever is going on in your thoughts right now is an activity of your soul. Your mind is engaged, your emotions are feeling certain things, and your will is making choices; that is the soul, the realm of experience.

When Luke says that these early Christians were united in both spirit and soul he means not only that they shared the life of Jesus as a fact of their existence, but also that they *experienced* it. That is what made the difference. Christians everywhere in the world are *already* united. Unity exists as a fact; it is the uniting of the body of Christ by the Holy Spirit. But these early Christians were united not only in heart (spirit) but also in soul; they emotionally enjoyed their unity. It was part of their daily life.

In many churches today there is unity, a oneness of spirit, but there is no experience of it in the soul. It is quite possible to come to church and sit together in the pews, united in a physical presence with other Christians, or to sing the same hymns and listen to the same message and relate to God individually, but to have no sense of body life, no sense of belonging to one another. This is what our younger generation is desperately trying to tell us. "There is no soul in your services," they say to the church at large; "There is no sense of oneness. You may belong to God, but you don't belong to each other." In the early church the believers' sense of belonging to one another manifested itself in a new attitude toward the material aspect of life. "No one said that any of the things which he possessed was his own"—that is, exclusively his. This is not Communism, for it is not a forced distribution of goods. It is not an attempt to make everyone give up their material things and redistribute them to others. No, it is a changed attitude, one which says, "Nothing I possess is for my exclusive use, but everything I possess is God's, and therefore it is available to anyone who needs it."

Making Life Visible

This is what the church ought to be like, and when it operates like this there will always be results. Luke summarizes them for us:

And with great power the apostles gave their testimony to the resurrection of the Lord Jesus (Acts 4:33).

Power in witness occurs whenever body life is present. God has designed that His church should operate as a body, and we can understand His design as we observe the proper functioning of the physical bodies in which we live. Our life, the life of our spirit—our personality, if you like—can only be made manifest to others through the body. It takes the body to make the life visible. This is also true of the church. If the church of Jesus Christ is not functioning as a body, then the life that is in it (which is the life of Jesus) can never be seen.

Notice that although the power was focused in a few men, it

took the whole body of Christians (over five thousand by now), to make the power possible. The twelve apostles gave the witness, but the church was participating in their ministry and making their power possible.

Furthermore, Luke says, "Great grace was upon them all." What is grace? It is one of those terms we Christians use freely, yet with only a vague idea of what it means. But grace means something specific. It is a word that describes the enrichment of life that results from the love and power of God. Somebody has defined grace in the form of an acrostic:

*G*od's
*R*iches
*A*t
*C*hrist's
*E*xpense

The Law of Love

God's grace appeared in the early church in two ways. First, it produced sharing of wealth to meet needs, the bearing of one another's burdens. Paul puts it this way: "Bear one another's burdens, and so fulfil the law of Christ" (Gal. 6:2). The law of Christ is the basic expression of Christian living, the law of love. "A new commandment," Jesus said, "I give to you, that you love one another, even as I have loved you" (John 13:34). To love means to know someone. You cannot love someone you do not know. Until you know a person you cannot love him; you can only love your image of him.

Much of the frustration in Christian homes between parents and children arises because parents have an image of what they want their children to be, and that is what they love. Unless their children measure up to that particular image, they do not love them. If a child goes wrong, does not measure up to the standard, then the love ceases, because it is not directed toward the child as he *is,* but only to the image of what he *ought to be.* It is so important to understand this. Our Lord said that love is fundamental to Christian expression. It is the means by which men will know that we are believers, that God is true, and that Jesus is a Savior. "By this all men will know that you are my disciples, if you have love for one another" (John 13:35). The mark of Christian success is not activity or even morality, though these are an important part of Christian expression. But the primary and fundamental expression of Christian living is not that you stop doing wrong things; it is that you love one another, that you bear one another's burdens and so fulfil the law of Christ.

This is where the Christians of the early church began, and grace began to enrich their lives:

> There was not a needy person among them, for as many as were possessors of lands or houses sold them, and brought the proceeds of what was sold and laid it at the apostles' feet; and distribution was made to each as any had need (Acts 4:34,35).

In Philippians, Paul says concerning the Lord Jesus, ". . . .Who, though he was in the form of God, did not count equality with God a thing to be grasped" [that is, not a thing to be held onto, clutched, or clung to], "but emptied himself" [renounced his rights, stopped clinging to his prerogatives], "taking the form of a servant" (Phil. 2:6,7). That was the first step in relieving the need of a desperate world. Jesus did not regard His equality with God as something to be held onto. And the first step which we ourselves must take to rectify the desperate condition of society around us is to stop clinging to things.

Are you clinging to anything? To a certain material standard of living, to status, to personal ambition, or to something else? You will never be able to enter into and enjoy the life that flows in richness and fullness through the body of Christ until you let go. The man who clings is hanging on with clenched fists. But our Lord is pictured in almost every portrait with hands open, ready to give abundantly to those in need.

Son-of-a-Gift

The second form of grace—essential to body life—is the exercise of gifts.

Thus Joseph, who was surnamed by the apostles Barnabas (which means Son of Encouragement), a Levite, a native of Cyprus, sold a field which belonged to him, and brought the money and laid it at the apostles' feet (Acts 4:36,37).

In the body of Christ in Jerusalem there was a distribution of gifts by the Holy Spirit. These gifts (called "graces" in Ephesians 4) are described in First Corinthians 12 and Romans 12. The various gifts had been given by the Spirit to fulfill the ministry of the body in that particular place.

Among the early Christians was a man named Joseph. If I had used only his given name you would not have recognized him, but if I mention his nickname, you will know him immediately—Barnabas. He was the Barnabas of the open heart and the acceptant spirit, the Barnabas who encouraged young John Mark when he was humiliated and crushed by his failure in that first missionary visit of Paul's. Mark would probably have dropped out of Christian activity altogether if Barnabas had not found him and encouraged him, and then taken him on another trip to set him on his feet. This was the Barnabas who vouched for Saul after his conversion, after the new convert had come up to Jerusalem from Damascus. The other apostles were afraid of him, for Saul was the man who had been persecuting and killing the church.

Barnabas had the gift of exhortation, of comfort, of encouragement—a wonderful gift—which he used so diligently that everyone began to call him by his gift, the Son of Encouragement. That is true grace—through the exercise of gifts to sense and supply the needs of the body.

Cutting Off the Life

Beginning at Acts 5 we turn a corner. Now we start looking away from the character and nature of body life and instead start confronting the perils and dangers attached to it:

But a man named Ananias with his wife Sapphira sold a piece of property, and with his wife's knowledge he kept back some of the proceeds, and brought only a part and laid it at the apostles' feet. But Peter said, "Ananias, why has Satan filled your heart to lie to the Holy Spirit and to keep back part of the proceeds of the land? While it remained unsold, did it not remain your own? And after it was sold, was it not at your disposal? How is it that you have contrived this deed in your heart? You have not lied to men but to God." When Ananias heard these words, he fell down and died. And great fear came upon all who heard of it. The young men rose and wrapped him up and carried him out and buried him (Acts 5:1-6).

What is this account telling us? Here a man and his wife are earnestly wanting to have a part in what is going on, a piece of the action. They sold some property, just as Barnabas did, but they bring only part of the money to lay at the apostles' feet. Is there anything wrong with this? Not a thing. When Ananias comes to Peter the Apostle says to him, in effect, "Ananias, this land was yours to sell or to keep. You had the right to dispose of your property as you saw fit. And after it was sold you had every right to say what the money was to be used for." Well, then, what is wrong? Peter, exercising his gift of discernment, says to Ananias, "You have lied. It wasn't wrong for you to withhold some of the money, but then to ..ct as though you had given it all—that is what is wrong. You lied, you pretended. You're a sham, a phony." When that penetrating analysis hit the ears of Ananias, he dropped dead at Peter's feet.

His wife, we are told, had also been part of this process: "by his wife's knowledge" this deception had been enacted. The rest of the story follows:

After an interval of about three hours his wife came in, not knowing what had happened. And Peter said to her, "Tell me whether you sold the land for so much." And she said, "Yes, for so much." But Peter said to her, "How is it that you have agreed together to tempt the Spirit of the Lord? Hark, the feet of those that have buried your husband are at the door, and they will carry you out." Immediately she fell down at his feet and died. When the young men came in they found her dead, and they carried her out and buried her beside her husband.

And great fear came upon the whole church, and upon all who heard of these things (Acts 5:7-11).

There were three "greats" in the early church: great power, great grace, and great fear. Why did this terrible tragedy occur? Why was the Holy Spirit so severe? Is this what He always does with His church? No, it doesn't happen physically now, but this is a picture by which God teaches us a sharp and penetrating lesson. Just as the healing of the lame man pictures what the Lord Jesus does in the inner life of a person who knows and follows Him, so this judgment of God pictures what happens in a person's life when he indulges in pretense. The moment we pretend to be something we're not, we are immediately cut off from the flow of the life of Christ. This doesn't mean that we are no longer a Christian, but it means that instead of being part of a living, vital movement, we become dead and unresponsive cells in the body. Paralysis sets in throughout the area over which we have influence.

This story of Ananias and Sapphira underscores for us the result of our own hypocrisy. The minute they pretended to be something they were not—death! When we are with other Christians we often put on a mask of adequacy, but inside we are inadequate, and we know it. We are struggling with problems in our homes, but we don't want to tell anyone about them. We can't get along with our children, but we'll never admit it to anyone. Our pride keeps us from sharing what is going on between husbands and wives, and between parents and children. Somebody asks us how things are going. "Great, great! Fine!" "How's everything at home?" "Oh, wonderful! We're having a wonderful time!" The minute we say that, and it's not true, we die. Death sets in. And soon that death pervades the whole church. This kind of dishonesty is a primary characteristic of the church today.

To break through this death, to begin to share realistically with one another, the way is always the same: repent and believe. Acknowledge that you have been doing it wrong, and then understand that God has already given you, in Jesus Christ, all that it takes to do what you should. Then start opening up and sharing your burdens. You will start in a rather small way, perhaps, and it will be difficult at first. But it is the sharing of lives that makes power and grace to flow through the body.

We are concerned about the world around us, with its desperate sickness. The life of the church is not to be merely a religious hobby to which we give some time and attention when it suits us; the body life of the church is the very focus of the work of God to help change the structure and pattern of life all around us, to release salt into society and light into the darkness of the world. It must begin and increase by the understanding and experience of body life.

Chapter Eleven

Times of Peril

Acts 5:12-42

A helpful key in understanding God's teaching is to see that the visible, physical events recorded in Scripture illustrate invisible spiritual situations and forces. The visible event is occurring *because of* the unseen spiritual situation. This is what we must understand if we are going to face life and understand it properly. The Bible consistently stresses that you can never explain what happens in this world on the basis of an evaluation and assessment of visible things. You must look behind the visible to the invisible.

We come now to a series of events which center around the confrontation between the apostles and the Sanhedrin. In this section four factors are highlighted that will always be present whenever the church is operating in times of peril. If we are aware of the peril and stress of our own day, we can see that these four things are essential to our own lives. First, there is a clear demonstration of the power of God:

Now many signs and wonders were done among the people by the hands of the apostles. And they were all together in Solomon's Portico. None of the rest dared join them, but the people held them in high honor. And more than ever believers were added to the Lord, multitudes both of men and women, so that they even carried out the sick into the streets, and laid them on beds and pallets, that as Peter came by at least his shadow might fall on some of them. The people also gathered from the towns around Jerusalem, bringing the sick and those afflicted with unclean spirits, and they were all healed (Acts 5:12-16).

This sounds like the days of Jesus all over again, doesn't it? Here is a tremendous display of physical healing power at the hands of the apostles, resulting in multitudes of believers being added to the church. No one knows how many, but it may have been ten thousand or more in this city with a normal population of about forty or fifty thousand. Here is an obvious evidence of the power of God at work.

Striking Powers

But many people today are troubled by this account. They say, "What's wrong with the church today? Why don't we have signs and wonders and mighty events like these taking place in our own day?" Many faith healers, in trying to reproduce these signs and wonders, succeed only in a temporary restoration, due to a psychological effect in the afflicted. Nevertheless, many people feel that the church is not living in power unless these physical miracles are present.

But notice some things that Luke carefully points out to us. First, he says, these healings were not done by the believers in general, but by *the hands of the apostles.* These men, gathered together in Solomon's Porch, were obviously anointed by God with unusual and striking powers—powers for which the apostles had prayed after being released by the Jewish rulers (Acts 4: 29,30). They had asked God to work through them with signs and wonders, and that is exactly what He did. As we have noted earlier, these were the signs that identified the apostles. They were never intended for the church at large. They were intended to confirm the ministry of these mighty apostles, who laid the foundation of the church in the giving of the Scriptures. Not only were they to manifest the power of God in physical ways, but this physical manifestation was to be a symbol of the spiritual power which God would release among the people.

What Greater Works?

It is always a mistake to put great emphasis on a physical miracle. Although miracles attract attention, they also tend to confuse people, so that ultimately the observers miss the point of what God is saying. That is why the Lord Jesus consistently said to the men and women whom He healed in the days of His flesh, "Now don't tell anybody about it." He didn't send the healed people out to broadcast the story; He said instead, "Go home and say nothing to anyone." Jesus did not want the confusing effect of physical miracles to thwart His spiritual ministry.

That is exactly what happened here in Acts. We read that when the apostles began to heal the sick, cast out demons, and relieve those who were distressed, the multitudes "carried out the sick into the streets and laid them on beds and pallets, that as Peter came by at least his shadow might fall on some of them" (Acts 5:15). This is a manifestation of the superstition that immediately begins to develop when physical miracles occur. There is nothing here to suggest that the apostles encouraged this kind of thing at all. Nor does it say that Peter's shadow *did* heal them.

Jesus had said, "He who believes in me will also do the works that I do" (John 14:12). Those words were spoken to the apostles, and here they are, doing the same works that Jesus did, the same miracles of healing. "And," said Jesus, "greater works than these will he do." Greater works than physical healing? What greater works? Why, *spiritual* healings. God wants most of all to heal the hurt in man's *spirit*. That is where the problem really lies. Every person ever healed by the Lord Jesus or by the disciples in the days of the early church eventually died. But when God heals the spirit, it is an eternal event.

The physical power displayed here is a symbol and guarantee of the spiritual power available to the church at all times. I don't mean that God has stopped all physical healing; He has not. But the deepest need of man is *spiritual* healing, not physical. And the power of God to heal spiritually is still present and available to us. And when this spiritual healing happens, multitudes will be added to the church.

Not Bound — *W and is Not Bound* —

The (second) significant factor in this account follows immediately:

> But the high priest rose up and all who were with him, that is, the party of the Sadducees, and, filled with jealousy, they arrested the apostles and put them in the common prison. But at night an angel of the Lord opened the prison doors and brought them out and said, "Go and stand in the temple and speak to the people all the words of this Life." And when they heard this, they entered the temple at daybreak and taught (Acts 5:17-21).

Then follows one of the classic examples of doubletake in all of history:

> Now the high priest came and those who were with him and called together the council and all the senate of Israel, and sent to the prison to have them brought. But when the officers came, they did not find them in the prison, and they returned and reported, "We found the prison securely locked and the sentries standing at the doors, but when we opened it we found no one inside." Now when the captain of the temple and the chief priests heard these words, they were much perplexed about them, wondering what this would come to. And someone came and told them, "The men whom you put in prison are standing in the temple and teaching the people." Then the captain with the officers went and brought them, but without violence, for they were afraid of being stoned by the people (Acts 5:21-26).

What lesson is God trying to teach us here? Why, that there is a liberty in the Spirit which nothing that man can do will ever touch. "Where the Spirit of the Lord is, there is freedom" (2 Cor. 3:17). It is no problem for God to get a man out of jail. He doesn't even have to go through a bail bondsman—He simply sends an angel! He can even send an earthquake, as He did for Paul and Silas at Philippi.

But it is also clear from events later on in Acts and in church history that God does not always intend to get His people physically out of prison. The point of the story is—as Paul beautifully put it in another place—that the Word of God is not bound. The resurrection power of a living God cannot be held by prison walls, gates, bars, and chains. You cannot hinder the preaching and teaching of the Word of God with prisons.

Behind the Opposition

As we go on, the third factor emerges:

And when they had brought them, they set them before the council. And the high priest questioned them, saying, "We strictly charged you not to teach in this name, yet here you have filled Jerusalem with your teaching and you intend to bring this man's blood upon us." But Peter and the apostles answered, "We must obey God rather than men. The God of our fathers raised Jesus, whom you killed by hanging him on a tree. God exalted him at his right hand as Leader and Savior, to give repentance to Israel and forgiveness of sins. And we are witnesses to these things, and so is the Holy Spirit, whom God has given to those who obey him." When they heard this they were enraged and wanted to kill them (Acts 5:27-33).

This last statement sounds familiar, doesn't it? Peter and the other apostles simply told these men the truth. They stood before them and very quietly said, "Look. The God of our fathers raised up Jesus, whom you killed." That is a clear statement of fact. "God has exalted Him at His right hand as Leader and Savior, to give repentance to Israel and forgiveness of sins." This is another statement of fact. "And we are witnesses to these things, and so is the Holy Spirit." With that simple statement of clear, plain truth, these rulers became violent and set out to kill the apostles.

This reaction shows clearly the fallen nature of man. Man is in the grip of forces beyond his knowledge and ken, evil forces which are implacably opposed to the will, purpose, and love of God. Whenever truth is uttered it enrages men like this. They oppose it with the only weapon they can think of—physical violence. Wherever the gospel goes, it not only invites and redeems some people, but it also enrages others. But beyond this immediate opposition of men is the opposition of certain malevolent beings; as Paul says, "We are not contending against flesh and blood" (since it is not men who are ultimately the problem)," . . . but against principalities, against the powers . . . against the spiritual hosts of wickedness in the heavenly places" (Eph. 6:12). This is where the opposition and hostility is ultimately coming from.

That is why it is so useless to attempt physical resistance against these kinds of forces. What good does it do to kill and burn and destroy those who are the puppets of evil forces? They will only raise up other men and use them in their place. What advantage is gained by wiping out at the polls groups of people who are opposed to something that God wants done? The evil forces will only raise up other men and women to do it all over again. What God wants to get across to His people is that they will never do any real good until they attack the *spiritual* forces. God has placed in our hands the spiritual equipment to do so. The next verses of the passage illustrate this:

> But a Pharisee in the council named Gamaliel, a teacher of the law, held in honor by all the people, stood up and ordered the men to be put outside for a while. And he said to them, "Men of Israel, take care what you do with these men. For before these days Theudas arose, giving himself out to be somebody, and a number of men, about four hundred, joined him; but he was slain, and all who followed him were dispersed and came to nothing. After him Judas the Galilean arose in the days of the census and drew away some of the people after him; he also perished, and all who followed him were scattered. So in

the present case I tell you, keep away from these men and let them alone; for if this plan or this undertaking is of men, it will fail; but if it is of God, you will not be able to overthrow them. You might even be found opposing God!" So they took his advice . . . (Acts 5:34-40).

Here the apostles are confronted with the same group that had just murdered their Lord, threatened by the same hostility that had accomplished the death of Jesus. Their lives are at stake. Why didn't these rulers kill them? Surely the apostles could not have predicted how God would deliver them. They had no way of knowing that there was seated on that very council a man with a calmer frame of mind, who would listen to reason and lay a quieting hand upon these tumultuous passions. But God knew. And God knew how to use that man and when to have him speak. Although these were men controlled by evil forces, they were also subject to the overriding sovereignty of the Holy Spirit.

Worthy to Suffer

The account closes with one additional event:

So they took his advice, and when they had called in the apostles, they beat them and charged them not to speak in the name of Jesus, and let them go. Then they left the presence of the council, rejoicing that they were counted worthy to suffer dishonor for the name. And every day in the temple and at home they did not cease teaching and preaching Jesus as the Christ (Acts 5:40-42).

I love that: "They did not cease." In fact, they counted themselves fortunate to suffer dishonor for Jesus' name. When we were called to be a Christian we were called to suffer. As Paul said in his Letter to the Philippians, "It has been granted to you that . . . you should not only believe in him but also suffer for his sake" (Phil. 1:29). Suffering is an integral part of the Christian experience. "Do not be surprised at the fiery ordeal which comes upon you to prove you, as though something strange were happening to you" (1 Pet. 4:12). You go through heartaches, disappointments, and ostracism, all for the sake of "the Name." Don't think this is strange. It is the privilege to which we are called.

What else can we expect if we stand for the truth in a world run by illusion? When a normal person lives in a world full of oddballs they think *he* is odd. But that is the suffering to which the Christian is called. Like these disciples, we ought to thank God for it and rejoice in it. Jesus said that, didn't He?

Blessed are you when men revile you and persecute you and utter all kinds of evil against you falsely on my account. Rejoice and be glad, for your reward is great in heaven, for so men persecuted the prophets who were before you (Matt. 5:11).

Chapter Twelve

Seven Choice Men

Acts 6:1-8

In the parable of the wheat and the tares the Lord Jesus said that He, the Son of Man, would begin by sowing the field of the world with people who had the life of God in them, the sons of the kingdom. But shortly after this certain signs of evil, put there by the Devil, would appear. The Devil would sow weeds that would spring up right in the middle of the wheat.

In the Book of Acts we see the historical fulfillment of Jesus' prediction. First we see the wheat springing up in the midst of the world—men and women filled with the Spirit of God and equipped by the Spirit with gifts of ministry. In trust and dependence on the life of God in them they have tremendous impact on the city of Jerusalem. Then, in the deceit practiced by Ananias and Sapphira, there is the first indication of evil sown by the Devil. Although their dishonesty brings death into the church, it is met by the honesty and judgment of the Spirit of God.

Attack from Within

The second evidence of the weeds of the Devil's sowing is found in Acts 6, in this story of dissension—an attempt on the enemy's part to divide the church by envy and misunderstanding:

112

Now in these days, when the disciples were increasing in number, the Hellenists murmured against the Hebrews because their widows were neglected in the daily distribution (Acts 6:1).

In the early church in Jerusalem there were two kinds of Jews who had become Christians by faith in Jesus Christ. Some had been born and raised in provinces away from Palestine, so they had not learned Hebrew, but spoke Greek. Then there were those who were raised in Jerusalem and spoke Aramaic, a form of Hebrew. So the early church was divided, interestingly enough, by the language barrier between Greek and Hebrew.

Every day a distribution was made to the widows who were in need. A common fund was provided, out of which money was taken every day to meet the needs of the widows among the group, because they had no other means of support. Some inequity arose (whether deliberate or not is hard to tell, but it was very likely not deliberate), and it became the cause of the first dissension in the church.

The Hellenists expressed their dissatisfaction by murmuring, and murmuring is always deadly. These Greek-speaking Christians did not complain to those in authority, those responsible; they simply complained among themselves, thus spreading discontent throughout the whole body of Christians. When you complain about a problem to people who are not in a position to do much about it, that is murmuring. Murmuring brought the judgment of God upon the children of Israel in the wilderness in Old Testament days. Murmuring is always the mark of a querulous, discontented, unhappy spirit.

According to the Gift

Somehow the apostles heard of the murmuring—rumors travel fast—and when they heard they acted:

And the twelve summoned the body of the disciples and said,

"It is not right that we should give up preaching the word of God to serve tables. Therefore, brethren, pick out from among you seven men of good repute, full of the Spirit and of wisdom, whom we may appoint to this duty. But we will devote ourselves to prayer and to the ministry of the word" (Acts 6:2-4).

It almost looks as though the apostles were saying, "We're too good to serve tables. After all, we're apostles. Let's pick out seven flunkies who can do that, while we devote ourselves to the tremendously spiritual work of prayer and preaching the Word." But that would be to completely misread this passage. Remember that these apostles had been in the upper room with the Lord Jesus. They had seen him divest Himself of his garments, gird Himself with a towel, take a basin of water, and wash their dirty feet. They had heard His words, "He who is greatest among you shall be your servant" (Matt. 23:11). So the apostles were not in any sense downgrading the ministry of serving tables. They made this decision simply on the basis of a difference in spiritual gifts. Here is a very clear example of how the early church assigned duties on the basis of the distribution of gifts by the Holy Spirit.

The glory of this church was that they were conscious of the superintendency of the Holy Spirit, aware that the Lord Jesus Himself, by means of the Spirit, was the Head of the church. He was apportioning gifts, giving certain ministries to various individuals and sending them out with His own orders. All through the Book of Acts you can see a tremendous display of the directing power of the Holy Spirit.

The apostles understood then, according to their gift, that they were to lay the foundation of the church, for it was given to the apostles to lay foundations. That foundation is the Scriptures. It is on the Scriptures that the church rests. Whenever the church has rested on the foundation laid by the apostles, the truth as it is in Jesus, the church has always had strength, power, and grace.

Therefore, it was most necessary that the apostles give themselves to the ministry of apostleship, which involved "prayer and the ministry of the word." As they met together in prayer they learned and understood the mind of God. The Spirit of God reminded them of what the Lord Jesus had taught them, and they in turn imparted this to the church. At that time the Scriptures as we have them had not yet been written. Yet all the truths contained in our New Testament were being uttered by the apostles as they went about teaching the people.

But they recognized that other men and women in this vast congregation also had gifts—gifts which would qualify them to do this kind of work. So the apostles said, in effect, "We are simply sticking with the gifts that were given to us, and we want you to find among yourselves those who have other gifts." So they charged the congregation to elect from among themselves seven men who had the gifts appropriate to the problem.

Specifications

There were several qualifications which the congregation was to look for. First, the people chosen were to be men, not women. And second, they were to be believers. The church never has any reason to go to the world for help in carrying on the life of the body. The Holy Spirit has adequately equipped the body of Christ to do all that it needs to do. This may appear obvious, but in the matter of fund-raising, at least, many churches make the mistake of relying upon secular organizations, which is a denial of the life of the body.

The third qualification was that they were to be "men of good reputation," men of good character who could be trusted, who had already won the confidence of others. Fourth, they were to be spiritual men. Now what does this mean? The word "spiritual" is one of the most misunderstood in the whole Bible. Is a spiritual person one who goes around mouthing pious sayings, using every situation to quote a verse of Scripture? Is this a truly spiritual person? No, according to the New Testament a spiritual person is a normal person, a person as God intended people to be.

Spirituality is dependence on the activity of God, a recognition that God is within you and that He intends to work through you, and that you expect Him to do it. The opposite of spiritual

ity is carnality. A carnal Christian is one who counts on something within himself. He may be ready to give up his sleep, his
wealth, and his girl friend to serve God, but if he is not resting on
Christ he is still carnal. These men had to be spiritual men.

Fifth, they had to have the gift of wisdom. They were to be
"full of the Spirit and of wisdom," to be able to apply Scriptural
knowledge to a practical situation. That is what these men were
to do. They had a problem. There was an inequity of distribution
caused perhaps by neglect, or by a lack of concern, or by some
technical problem that made the distribution difficult. Whatever
the reason, it required the application of truth, so men were
needed who knew how to take truth and apply it to a specific
situation.

These men were to be chosen on this basis. The apostles gave
the church this charge, and the church carried it out:

> And what they said pleased the whole multitude, and they
> chose Stephen, a man full of faith and of the Holy Spirit, and
> Philip, and Prochorus, and Nicanor, and Timon, and Parmenas,
> and Nicolaus, a proselyte of Antioch. These they set before
> the apostles, and they prayed and laid their hands upon them
> (Acts 6:5,6).

There is something wonderful here. Every one of these names is
Greek, which means that the men chosen were probably all from
among the complaining party, the Greek-speaking Jews. When the
far larger group of Hebrew-speaking Christians were asked to
choose men, they chose them from the very group that was
issuing the complaint. And that ended the dissension. They entrusted these men with the responsibility of resolving the problem
within their own ranks, thus indicating their trust of them and of
their ability to solve this problem in the Lord.

Sharing the Ministry

Evidently these men were elected by the congregation and
were then called before the apostles, who laid their hands upon

them, thus identifying themselves with their ministries. In the Old Testament, whenever a Hebrew brought an animal to be sacrificed he first laid his hands upon it, by which he said, "This animal and I are identified. My sins are laid upon him and his blood shed for me is as though my own blood were being shed."

In the New Testament this was carried on into the body of Christ as an act of identification. These apostles were saying, "These seven men whom you have chosen, who have the gifts and the qualifications we outlined, are part of our ministry as apostles, and we are part of theirs. We belong in the body together, and in the body every gift is important." Paul writes,

For the body does not consist of one member, but of many. . . . The eye cannot say to the hand, "I have no need of you," nor again the head to the feet, "I have no need of you" (1 Cor. 12:14, 21).

The members are interdependent, one upon another. If we do not understand and recognize that every member of the body has been given a gift, and unless each member begins to exercise his gift, the body will suffer. As Paul says, "If one member suffers, all suffer together; if one member is honoured, all rejoice together" (1 Cor. 12:26). What the apostles are seeking to demonstrate is the identification of the members of the body with one another. Those with leadership gifts are equal, they say, with those who serve tables. Each gift is absolutely essential to the operation of the body.

A situation that recently developed in a nearby church illustrates this principle well. A sizable number of converts were joining the church, all from one particular geographical area. The church elders became curious and found that one of their members was a milkman in the area. He was witnessing widely to people during the course of his work and was winning them to Christ, because he had the gift of an evangelist and he loved the Lord. He did not realize that he had any ties to the rest of the body, but he was witnessing and reaching others and winning them to Christ.

One day a number of the church leaders called him in and said, "Look; we've been watching you and we see that you have the gift of an evangelist. We want to show you that you're not alone, but that we're all one body with you. We want to identify with you." So they had a little service and asked the man to kneel, and they all came and laid their hands on him and prayed for him and thus expressed this great truth: we are members one of another. This man was tremendously touched. Tears rolled down his face as he stood and thanked them for their identification with him in the body of Christ.

Evidence of Life

The healing of the dissension in the church and the flowing of body life yielded four immediate results. First,

And the word of God increased.... (Acts 6:7a).

This phrase is used several times in Scripture, and every time it means that the Word was more widely proclaimed. Obviously the apostles now had more time to speak, to utter the words of God, the mind of the Spirit. Second, as a direct result of this ministry,

The number of the disciples multiplied greatly in Jerusalem (Acts 6:7b).

All we need to do is to get the truth out to people. The Bible speaks the truth; it reveals the way things really are. We are living in a world ruled by illusion and fantasy, where people are confused, disturbed, and upset. In minds that are groping for reality the truth hits with wonderful impact. There is an immediate awareness, as there was in Jesus' days on earth, that what is being said is true. Disciples multiply because men and women are drawn to the truth; they want to know what is right and what is real. And the third result:

A great many of the priests were obedient to the faith (Acts 6:7c).

This is wonderful. The priests were men who were active all day long in religious ritual; they had to kill the animals that were offered as sacrifices on the altars of the temple. They were religious people performing ritualistic observances. But now, as the truth about Jesus was set before them, something was happening. They were discovering that Jesus was the key to their ritual, that all these sacrifices pointed to Him. Finally,

Stephen, full of grace and power, did great wonders and signs among the people (Acts 6:8).

Stephen became the first martyr. The next chapter is devoted completely to the message he preached, the longest sermon in the Book of Acts. At the close of it the enraged hearers stoned Stephen to death because of his testimony to the truth. And in Chapter 8 we read of Philip, another one of these seven men, who also did great signs and wonders.

Neither Philip nor Stephen did signs and wonders until after the laying on of hands by the apostles, which indicates that in some sense the ministry of these deacons (and later of the elders of the church) was an apostolic ministry. They did these great signs and wonders as a result of having been identified with the work of the apostles.

The second thing to be noted is that these signs were to confirm the introduction of new things in the church. When the apostles first began to proclaim the gospel of the resurrected Lord it was confirmed to the people by signs and wonders. As the apostles now extended their ministry to include others with gifts within the church, this too was confirmed with signs and wonders.

The Word of God makes clear that these mighty miracles were particularly slanted toward the Jewish mind, that they were given specifically for the purpose of confirming something which was being introduced for the first time. The miracles did not continue in the church, and they do not continue to this day. This doesn't mean that God is unable to do miracles. He can and does do them. But they are no longer in the nature of physical signs and wonders. These were reserved for the initial experiences of the early Christians as they introduced God's truth to the world.

Chapter Thirteen

The Issue is Jesus

Acts 6:8-8:1

We come now to the story of Stephen, one of the seven men who had been chosen by the congregation of the early church to be apostolic helpers:

> And Stephen, full of grace and power, did great wonders and signs among the people. Then some of those who belonged to the synagogue of the Freedmen (as it was called), and of the Cyrenians, and of the Alexandrians, and of those from Cilicia and Asia, arose and disputed with Stephen. But they could not withstand the wisdom and the Spirit with which he spoke. Then they secretly instigated men who said, "We have heard him speak blasphemous words against Moses and God." And they stirred up the people and the elders and the scribes, and they came upon him and seized him and brought him before the council, and set up false witnesses, who said, "This man never ceases to speak words against this holy place and the law; for we have heard him say that this Jesus of Nazareth will destroy this place, and will change the customs which Moses delivered to us." And, gazing at him, all who sat in the council saw that his face was like the face of an angel (Acts 6:8-15).

Stephen, you remember, was one of those Greek-speaking Jews called Hellenists, having been born in another country and speaking Greek instead of Hebrew or Aramaic. In the city of Jerusalem were a number of synagogues that had been formed by Greek-

speaking Jews from various parts of the world. To these synagogues Stephen evidently went and preached in Greek, giving
testimony to his faith in Jesus Christ. Five of these synagogues
are mentioned in this passage. One was the Synagogue of the
Freedmen, founded by Jews who had been slaves in the Roman
Empire and had later been set free. Then there were two groups
from Africa: the synagogues of the Cyrenians and of the Alex-
andrians. There were also two groups from what we presently call
Turkey: Cilicia and Asia, two of the Roman provinces of that
day.

It is interesting to note that the capital of Cilicia was Tarsus,
and undoubtedly a young man named Saul was among those who
disputed with Stephen when he came to the Cilician synagogue
preaching Jesus Christ. Saul was among those men of whom it is
said here, "But they could not withstand the wisdom and the
Spirit with which he [Stephen] spoke." This brilliant young Jew,
Saul of Tarsus, was later to become the Apostle Paul. But now he
arose and disputed, yet he could not answer Stephen. That must
have been a blow to his pride, since Saul prided himself as an
authority on the Scriptures; after all, he sat at the feet of the
great teacher, Gamaliel!

When these men could not answer Stephen they set out to
charge him officially before the court, and to find false witnesses
to testify that he had blasphemed Moses and God. (It is interesting that they put Moses first, making him more important than
God!) Then they stirred up the people and the elders and the
scribes, and they seized Stephen in order to bring him before the
council.

Charge and Countercharge

So here is Stephen, standing before the same Sanhedrin that
had condemned the Lord Jesus to death and had just experienced
such difficulty with Peter and John and the other apostles. By the
time Stephen came before the council the official charges had
been narrowed to two very specific offenses: that he was saying

threatening things against the temple ("This man never ceases to speak words against this holy place. . . for we have heard him say that this Jesus of Nazareth will destory this place") and against the law ("and will change the customs which Moses delivered to us"). Stephen had probably said something very similar to what was alleged here, but he had not meant it to be taken that way. So it was impossible for him to answer with a simple yes or no when the high priest read him the official charges and asked, "Are these things so? How do you plead: guilty or not guilty?" Stephen had to explain what he meant. He *had* said something about Jesus' coming, and that the worship of the temple was changed. He *had* said that the customs which Moses had given would be altered.

Therefore, in Stephen's brilliant defense of what he believed—really a review of the history of the people of Israel—he answers the two charges against him and he brings a charge of his own against the people. They had charged him with saying that Moses' teachings were to be changed (blasphemy!). Stephen answers by saying,

> This is the Moses who said to the Israelites, "God will raise up for you a prophet from your brethren, as he raised me up" (Acts 7:37).

Moses himself had said that things were going to be changed, that God was going to raise up another Prophet who, like himself, would speak to the people and give a whole new set of provisions for life from God. Then he answers the charge concerning the temple in a brief section toward the close of his message:

> Our fathers had the tent of witness in the wilderness, even as he who spoke to Moses directed him to make it, according to the pattern that he had seen. Our fathers in turn brought it in with Joshua when they dispossessed the nations which God thrust out before our fathers. So it was until the days of David, who found favor in the sight of God and asked leave to find a habitation for the God of Jacob. But it was Solomon who built a house for him. Yet the Most High does not dwell in houses made with hands; as the prophet says, "Heaven is my

throne, and earth my footstool. What house will you build for me, says the Lord, or what is the place of my rest? Did not my hand make all these things?" (Acts 7:44-50).

God Himself, through the prophet Isaiah, had predicted that the temple would not always be an adequate place to worship God. In fact, no building will ever be. God is bigger than buildings. God is the One who made all things, who makes the material from which a building is made, and who makes the men who put that building together. God has not intended that He should be worshiped in a building made with hands. Isaiah said that, not Stephen. And so he successfully answers this charge.

Then Stephen levels a charge against his hearers. He says, in effect, that far from following the great men of faith whom they professed to admire and revere, they were actually identifying themselves with the godless and idolatrous forces that had consistently opposed these men, and had even put them to death on many occasions. To illustrate his point, he selects from the course of Israel's history three outstanding heroes of faith and indicates the contrast between them and his listeners.

Pointed Contrasts

Notice how this mighty preacher of the early church developed his thesis. He begins with Abraham, the first of the three figures:

And the high priest said, "Is this so?" And Stephen said, "Brethren and fathers, hear me. The God of glory appeared to our father Abraham when he was in Mesopotamia, before he lived in Haran, and said to him, 'Depart from your land and from your kindred and go into the land which I will show you.' Then he departed from the land of the Chaldeans and lived in Haran. And after his father died, God removed him from there into this land in which you are now living; yet he gave him no inheritance in it, not even a foot's length, but promised to give it to him in possession and to his posterity after him, though he had no child. And God spoke to this effect, that his posterity would be aliens in a land belonging to others, who would enslave them and ill-treat them four hundred years. 'But I will judge the nation which they serve,' said God, 'and after that they shall come out and worship me in this place.' And he gave him the covenant of circumcision. And so Abraham became the father of Isaac, and circumcised him on the eighth day; and Isaac became the father of Jacob, and Jacob of the twelve patriarchs" (Acts 7:1-8).

Stephen is saying that Abraham was a man of lifelong faith, a man who dared to change his life pattern in obedience to God. He left his father's house and went out into a land he had never seen before, and although he never owned a foot of ground there, he nevertheless believed that God would do what He had said. Although Abraham had no child, he believed that God would give him descendants. Stephen is drawing a very pointed, unspoken contrast here. "Abraham your father," Stephen said, "was a man of faith who dared to make changes out of obedience to God."

The next man from their past is Joseph:

And the patriarchs, jealous of Joseph, sold him into Egypt; but God was with him, and rescued him out of all his afflictions, and gave him favor and wisdom before Pharaoh, king of Egypt, who made him governor over Egypt and over all his household. Now there came a famine throughout all Egypt and Canaan, and great affliction, and our fathers could find no food. But when Jacob heard that there was grain in Egypt, he sent forth our fathers the first time. And at the second visit Joseph made himself known to his brothers, and Joseph's family became known to Pharaoh. And Joseph sent and called to him Jacob his father and all his kindred, seventy-five souls; and Jacob went down into Egypt. And he died, himself and our fathers, and they were carried back to Shechem and laid in the tomb that Abraham had bought for a sum of silver from the sons of Hamor in Shechem (Acts 7:9-16).

Joseph was a man of integrity and truth who believed God. God took him through deep waters and dark places, but eventually He exalted and honored him and fulfilled His word to him in everything He promised. Because Joseph obeyed God, God fulfilled every letter of His word to him. Therefore Joseph presents another contrast with Stephen's accusers, who refuse to obey God simply because it will mean some changes in their lives.

Failure and Faith

Stephen spends most of his time on Moses, the third man of faith, whom he was charged with blaspheming. He first outlines the early part of Moses life:

> But as the time of the promise drew near, which God had granted to Abraham, the people grew and multiplied in Egypt till there arose over Egypt another king who had not known Joseph. He dealt craftily with our race and forced our fathers to expose their infants, that they might not be kept alive. At this time Moses was born, and was beautiful before God. And he was brought up for three months in his father's house; and when he was exposed, Pharaoh's daughter adopted him and brought him up as her own son. And Moses was instructed in all the wisdom of the Egyptians, and he was mighty in his words and deeds.

> When he was forty years old, it came into his heart to visit his brethren, the sons of Israel. And, seeing one of them being wronged, he defended the oppressed man and avenged him by striking the Egyptian. He supposed that his brethren understood that God was giving them deliverance by his hand, but they did not understand. And on the following day he appeared to them as they were quarreling and would have reconciled them, saying, "Men, you are brethren, why do you wrong each other?" But the man who was wronging his neighbor thrust him aside, saying, "Who made you a ruler and a judge over us? Do you want to kill me as you killed the Egyptian yesterday?" At this retort Moses fled and became an exile in the land of Midian, where he became the father of two sons (Acts 7:17-29).

You may ask, "Why did Stephen tell these stories to people who knew them by heart?" Because he wanted to remind them of something. They had said to him, "You are blaspheming Moses, the great leader, the infallible authority." But Stephen was saying, "Have you forgotten that Moses was a failure during the first 80 years of his life? Have you forgotten that when Moses acted on the basis of the human knowledge and resources he possessed he fell flat on his face, and that when he tried to deliver his people, instead of becoming a missionary to them (as he thought God had appointed him), he became a murderer and had to flee? Instead of being a deliverer he became a refugee. Moses was a failure when he did not act by faith." Then Stephen moves to the second stage:

> Now when forty years had passed, an angel appeared to him in the wilderness of Mount Sinai, in a flame of fire in a bush. When Moses saw it he wondered at the sight; and as he drew near to look, the voice of the Lord came, "I am the God of your fathers, the God of Abraham and of Isaac and of Jacob." And Moses trembled and did not dare to look. And the Lord said to him, "Take off the shoes from your feet, for the place where you are standing is holy ground. I have surely seen the ill-treatment of my people that are in Egypt and heard their groaning, and I have come down to deliver them. And now come, I will send you to Egypt."

> This Moses whom they refused, saying, "Who made you a ruler and a judge?" God sent as both ruler and deliverer by the hand of the angel that appeared to him in the bush (Acts 7:30-35).

Catch the argument now. "You want to follow Moses," he says. "Well, Moses failed when he walked by the sight of his own eyes and in the wisdom of his own mind. But when God appeared and empowered him and taught him the proper source of strength and authority, he was sent back to be a ruler and deliverer." Stephen is stressing this essential fact: the only Person worth following is God! When people act in faith toward God they have all the power of an omnipotent God behind them. But when they refuse to obey God they fall flat on their faces!

Then comes the third stage, by which Stephen drives home his point with a vengeance:

He led them out, having performed wonders and signs in Egypt and at the Red Sea, and in the wilderness for forty years. This is the Moses who said to the Israelites, "God will raise up for you a prophet from your brethren, as he raised me up." This is he who was in the congregation in the wilderness with the angel who spoke to him at Mount Sinai, and with our fathers; and he received living oracles to give to us. Our fathers refused to obey him, but thrust him aside, and in their hearts they turned to Egypt, saying to Aaron, "Make for us gods to go before us; as for this Moses who led us out from the land of Egypt, we do not know what has become of him." And they made a calf in those days, and offered a sacrifice to the idol and rejoiced in the works of their hands. But God turned and gave them over to worship the host of heaven, as it is written in the book of the prophets: "Did you offer to me slain beasts and sacrifices, forty years in the wilderness, O house of Israel? And you took up the tent of Moloch, and the star of the god Rephan, the figures which you made to worship; and I will remove you beyond Babylon" (Acts 7:36-43).

Stephen says that the people refused to obey Moses and so began that whole system of idolatrous worship which led God at last, centuries later, to disperse them into the country of Babylon for 70 years of captivity. As they turned from Moses and disobeyed him they fell into evil, idolatrous practices which were so wicked that God had to judge them. And, Stephen's point is, Moses *himself* had said that it would happen again: "God will raise up for you a Prophet like me, and Him you must hear." That Prophet would be Jesus, the very one Stephen's hearers are now rejecting. They are following exactly the course of their fathers.

The Two-Edged Sword

Here is Stephen's conclusion:

You stiff-necked people, uncircumcised in heart and ears, you always resist the Holy Spirit. . . (Acts 7:51).

These Jews would understand these terms. "Stiff-necked"— proud, stubborn, unwilling to bow their heads at all. "Uncircumcised in heart"—the foreskin of their heart had never been removed; there had been no exposure of their life to the grace and glory of God. They were defiled, yet they refused to repent.

> As your fathers did, so do you. Which of the prophets did not your fathers persecute? And they killed those who announced beforehand the coming of the Righteous One, whom you have now betrayed and murdered, you who received the law as delivered by angels and did not keep it (Acts 7:51-53).

What forthright truth this is! It was terribly hard to bear. These rulers of the Jews became so enraged that we read in the next verse,

> Now when they heard these things they were enraged, and they ground their teeth against him (Acts 7:54).

They gnashed their teeth. This is the effect that truth has. Truth never allows you to remain neutral, never leaves a middle ground; it always drives you to either one side or the other. As Jesus said repeatedly of His own ministry, "I have not come to bring peace, but a sword" (Matt. 10:34); "He who does not gather with me scatters" (Luke 11:23). Those who are *against* Him are causing divisions, fomenting factions, creating schisms, and scattering.

> But he, full of the Holy Spirit, gazed into heaven and saw the glory of God, and Jesus standing at the right hand of God; and he said, "Behold, I see the heavens opened, and the Son of man standing at the right hand of God" (Acts 7:55,56).

These are almost the identical words which Jesus Himself had used before this same group just a few weeks earlier. He had said, "You will see the Son of man sitting at the right hand of Power, and coming with the clouds of heaven" (Mark 14:62). When they heard Stephen say this they knew the issue was Jesus, not Stephen.

Faithful Unto Death

What do you do with Jesus of Nazareth? Stephen's hearers were condemned by their own Scriptures. There was not a word they could say against Stephen. They either had to crown Jesus or crucify Him again. They either had to kiss His feet or kill His servant. They chose to kill His servant.

But they cried out with a loud voice and stopped their ears and rushed together upon him. Then they cast him out of the city and stoned him; and the witnesses laid down their garments at the feet of a young man named Saul. And as they were stoning Stephen, he prayed, "Lord Jesus, receive my spirit." And he knelt down and cried with a loud voice, "Lord, do not hold this sin against them." And when he had said this, he fell asleep. And Saul was consenting to his death (Acts 7:57–8:1).

What a vivid picture! Stephen's eyes are opened right in the presence of the council to see the Lord Jesus standing at the right hand of the Father. It is my conviction that every believer who dies sees this event, that when a believer steps out of time into eternity the next event waiting for him is the coming of the Lord Jesus for His own. Here Stephen sees Jesus waiting to step out and receive Him in a few moments, when he will be taken out of the city and stoned to death. Stephen sees the sight that greets the eyes of all those who fall asleep in Jesus. And he prays to Him in words that echo those of Jesus Himself on the Cross. Jesus had prayed, "Father, forgive them, for they know not what they do." Stephen says, "Lord, do not hold this sin against them." And when he had said this, he fell asleep.

Twice in this account we read about young Saul of Tarsus. All the people who killed Stephen brought their garments to Saul for safe keeping while they were doing the stoning. Saul had voted against Stephen in the council, and now he was consenting to his death. But the idea which the Holy Spirit wants us to grasp from this account is this: the blood of the martyrs is the seed of the church. When the church suffers in this way it always grows immensely.

Out of the blood of Stephen there was brought to the church the heart and soul of the mighty Apostle to the Gentiles, the Apostle Paul. Paul never forgot this scene. It was etched in his mind and memory so deeply that when Jesus stopped him on his way to Damascus and said, "Saul, Saul . . . it hurts you to kick against the goads," it was doubtless this memory of Stephen that He was referring to. It was like a goad digging at young Saul's conscience, preparing his heart for that moment of conversion.

The Book of Acts is an unfinished book. In this day and age there may be some Christians who will be called, like Stephen, to lay down their lives for Jesus' sake. The opposition is sharpening and the hostility is emerging, more vicious, more furious, more enraged on every side. We may face in our own day a tremendous outpouring of the hostility of depraved hearts against the message of Jesus Christ and a persecution of its bearers. May God grant that, like Stephen, we will be faithful unto death.

Chapter Fourteen

God Has the Edge

Acts 8:1-24

Remember Jesus' words to His disciples just before He was taken out of their sight: "You shall be my witnesses in Jerusalem and in all Judea and Samaria and to the end of the earth" (Acts 1:8). So far in this account the gospel has been restricted to the city of Jerusalem, where the apostles and the entire body of believers were remaining. As we move into the next section of Acts we will see how God thrusts His people out into the world beyond Jerusalem—into Judea and Samaria.

The first period in the history of the early church closed with the story of Stephen's death at the hands of an enraged Sanhedrin, who could not tolerate the truth which he spoke. The men who stoned Stephen laid their garments at the feet of Saul of Tarsus. By this the Holy Spirit indicates to us that out of the death of Stephen came ultimately the preaching of the Apostle Paul. The Sanhedrin silenced a voice that was upsetting a city, but without realizing it they were awakening a new voice that would upset an empire. That is the way God works. God continually uses opposition to advance His cause. Read what happened after Stephen's death:

And on that day a great persecution arose against the church in Jerusalem; and they were all scattered throughout the region of Judea and Samaria except the apostles. Devout men buried Stephen and made great lamentation over him. But Saul

131

laid waste the church, and, entering house after house, he dragged off men and women and committed them to prison. Now those who were scattered went about preaching the word. Philip went down to a city of Samaria and proclaimed to them the Christ (Acts 8:1-5).

Notice that the paragraph begins with persecution and ends with proclamation. The persecution that arose over Stephen pressed these early Christians out of Jerusalem, squirting them into Judea and Samaria, where they began to preach the Word—all according to the program of God. This young man, Saul of Tarsus, was part of God's plan even before he became a Christian. Picture young Saul as he trys to stamp out this "heresy" with all the energy of his flesh—entering house after house, dragging off men and women, and committing them to prison. In the rage of a tortured conscience Saul tried through zealous activity to cover up his anxiety, emptiness, and hurt.

Yet God used Saul's rage to accomplish two things: He forced the church out of Jerusalem, amd He made the early church depend on the gifts which the Spirit distributed to *everyone,* instead of simply on the apostles' gifts. Luke is careful to tell us that those who were scattered abroad were ordinary, plain-vanilla Christians who nevertheless had gifts of the Spirit. But they would never have discovered their gifts if God had not used this pressure to place them in circumstances where they had to develop the gifts of evangelism, witnessing, helps, wisdom, knowledge, teaching, and prophecy—all gifts which the Spirit had made available to them.

The Real Thing

The first mark of the way God works in resurrection power is that persecution leads to a wider proclamation of the truth. Let's pick up the account in Samaria:

And the multitudes with one accord gave heed to what was said by Philip, when they heard him and saw the signs which he did. For unclean spirits came out of many who were possessed, crying with a loud voice; and many who were paralyzed or lame were healed. So there was much joy in that city (Acts 8:6-8).

Here is the ministry of Philip, a layman. Yet it is a ministry of power, the power of the Holy Spirit. The result was a marvelous demonstration of what Christianity is like. In this brief paragraph there are three marks that always accompany a genuine ministry of the Spirit. The first is the ring of truth. Notice that it says, "The multitudes with one accord *gave heed* to what was said by Philip" (verse 6). When a great crowd of people listens intently, it is because they are struck by a note of reality. This was the way Jesus taught. He didn't teach the way the scribes and Pharisees did with quotations from other authorities, but He spoke with words that hit people as the truth and convicted them deep inside. As Philip talked this way people also stopped and listened. The second mark is the accompaniment of power:

For unclean spirits came out of many who were possessed, crying with a loud voice; and many who were paralyzed or lame were healed (Acts 8:7).

The power that delivers was manifest in Samaria as soon as Philip preached there. These miracles—the freeing from demonic spirits, the healings—were evidences of the power of God manifested on a visible and physical level, to help the people understand that God would also free them in the spirit. They were a demonstration of God's power to heal, both physically and spiritually. Wherever the gospel goes, it gives liberty.

And the third mark is joy:

So there was much joy in that city (Acts 8:8).

Our American cities are for the most part seething pools of human misery. Millions of people are living in squalor and poverty, in filth and degradation. Within them there is loneliness, emptiness, and depression of spirit. What can set them free? What can fill them with joy? The glory of the gospel is that wherever it goes, even though it may not immediately change people's outward circumstances, it does fill people with joy. And soon the circumstance begins to change as well.

Counterfeit Christianity

But notice the contrast in the next paragraph:

> But there was a man named Simon who had previously practiced magic in the city and amazed the nation of Samaria, saying that he himself was somebody great. They all gave heed to him, from the least to the greatest, saying, "This man is that power of God which is called Great." And they gave heed to him, because for a long time he had amazed them with his magic. But when they believed Philip as he preached good news about the kingdom of God and the name of Jesus Christ, they were baptized, both men and women. Even Simon himself believed, and after being baptized he continued with Philip. And, seeing signs and great miracles performed, he was amazed (Acts 8:9-13).

In this section the Holy Spirit deliberately contrasts the marks of authentic Christianity with those of a false and counterfeit faith. This is the third occasion in the Book of Acts of the sprouting of the Devil's seed. The first was the hypocrisy of Ananias and Sapphira, the second was the dissension which arose among the disciples when they quarreled over the distribution of goods to the widows, and the third is this manifestation of religious falseness through Simon the magician.

Notice the characteristics of this false religiosity. The primary feature by which this kind of religious falseness can be recognized is given to us right away:

> There was a man named Simon who had previously practiced magic in the city and amazed the nation of Samaria, saying that *he himself* was somebody great (Acts 8:9).

All false faith involves the inflation of an individual, usually by self-aggrandizement. But genuine Christianity makes little of the individual. "For what we preach is not ourselves," says the Apostle Paul, "but Jesus Christ as Lord, with ourselves as your servants for Jesus' sake" (2 Cor. 4:5). But here in Acts we have a man who exalted himself.

A popular faith healer I once listened to started out well: he took his text from Scripture, he began to develop it well, and I began to think I had been wrong about this man—until he came to the conclusion! Rather than giving an invitation to the thousands who were present to come to know Jesus Christ, this is what he said: "If you want to know God, then have faith in *my* prayers." The whole direction of his message was toward himself and his prayer.

False Christianity always attempts to interject a mediator between a believer and his God. But, "there is one mediator between God and men, the man Christ Jesus" (1 Tim. 2:5). There is none other. Counterfeit Christianity tries to insert someone who has an "in" with God, someone who has a special channel to God that other people don't have. When you hear that sort of thing you know that you are hearing the same kind of false Christianity that appeared here in the Book of Acts.

The second mark of false Christianity is a wide following, a widespread delusion:

> They all gave heed to him, from the least to the greatest, saying, "This man is that power of God which is called Great" (Acts 8:10).

These people thought God was so removed, so distant, that He would never appear Himself, but would only send His "power," as though the "power of God" were a different personality from God Himself! The whole city believed this delusion, from the least to the greatest. Similarly, the leaders of false cults today point to the numbers that follow them and say, "Look at all the people who believe in us. Fifty million Frenchmen can't be wrong!" But one of the chief characteristics of a false faith is that it can mislead the masses. These false leaders always have great followings.

The third mark is that of a counterfeit power:

And they gave heed to him, because for a long time he had amazed them with his magic (Acts 8:11).

In Scripture the term "magic" does not refer to sleight-of-hand tricks done before an audience. It applies instead to the occult practices of people who have somehow established a relationship with demonic powers and are being used by these powers to accomplish apparently wholesome miracles which cannot at first be distinguished from the real thing. But they never last. That is the mark of their falseness—diseases will reappear, symptoms will return, the miracle will fade.

When Moses appeared in Pharaoh's court and threw his staff down, it became a serpent. When he picked it up again, it became a staff. Immediately the magicians of Pharaoh's court threw their staffs down, and these also became serpents, apparently equalling the power of Moses. But then God told Moses to throw his staff down again. This time it became a serpent which ate up the other serpents! God always has an edge.

We are seeing the return of the occult in our own day. Thirty years ago people would have laughed if you had suggested that intelligent, educated people would believe in witches and warlocks, astrology and horoscopes. But now these beliefs are here, and we are going to see much more of them in the days to come. If you believe only what you see, you will be swept right along with what appear to be genuine miracles. But they are false and temporary, done by a counterfeit power.

The Devil Joins the Church

Here is the fourth mark of false Christianity:

Even Simon himself believed, and, after being baptized, he continued with Philip. And, seeing signs and great miracles performed, he was amazed (Acts 8:13).

The Devil must have been the first one who ever said, "If you can't lick 'em, join 'em." That is exactly what Simon did. If this were the only statement about Simon in the Scriptures, we would have to conclude that he had become a Christian, because the language used to describe him is the same as that used for genuine believers. "Simon himself believed and was baptized." He took upon himself the symbol of identification with Jesus Christ, thus openly joining this company who said they belonged to Jesus. But the rest of the account makes it clear that this man was a fraud. He said the right words and did the right things, and he was baptized. Yet he was unchanged; his heart was unregenerate.

As the account continues we see how God the Holy Spirit, working in power through His people, can expose this kind of fraud:

> Now when the apostles at Jerusalem heard that Samaria had received the word of God, they sent to them Peter and John, who came down and prayed for them that they might receive the Holy Spirit; for it had not yet fallen on any of them, but they had only been baptized in the name of the Lord Jesus. Then they laid their hands on them and they received the Holy Spirit. Now when Simon saw that the Spirit was given through the laying on of the apostles' hands, he offered them money, saying, "Give me also this power, that any one on whom I lay my hands may receive the Holy Spirit." But Peter said to him, "Your silver perish with you, because you thought you could obtain the gift of God with money! You have neither part nor lot in this matter, for your heart is not right before God. Repent therefore of this wickedness of yours, and pray to the Lord that, if possible, the intent of your heart may be forgiven you. For I see that you are in the gall of bitterness and in the bond of iniquity." And Simon answered, "Pray for me to the Lord, that nothing of what you have said may come upon me" (Acts 8:14-24).

Here again is the genuine manifestation of authentic Christianity—the coming of the Holy Spirit. But it says of these believers in Samaria that the Holy Spirit had not yet fallen on them. Well, then, what *had* happened? They had believed and had been baptized, so what had happened? Can a person become a Christian without the Holy Spirit?

Into One Body

We must be very careful in reading these verses to notice exactly what these Samaritan believers had and what they did not have. They did have power. The Holy Spirit was in their midst in power, setting them free from the illnesses and depressions that had been besetting them. And they had joy—the kind of joy that can never be produced except by the Holy Spirit. Power is an outward sign, while joy is inward. Both outwardly and inwardly these Samaritan believers were demonstrating the presence of the Holy Spirit in their lives. They were regenerate. They had been baptized in water as a testimony to that very regeneration which had occurred within their hearts and which manifested itself in the joy that was there. So we would make a great mistake if we said that the Holy Spirit was not yet in Samaria. He was, but what the account specifically says is that the Holy Spirit had not yet *fallen* upon them. The Holy Spirit does a great variety of different things, and this account makes clear that these believers had not yet received a certain manifestation of the Spirit. What was this manifestation?

These Christians had not yet been baptized by the Spirit *into one body*. They were still separate, individual, regenerated Christians—just as the apostles themselves had been before the Day of Pentecost. On that day they were baptized into a body and made members of one another. They became members of one body in Jesus Christ at the same time that they received the gifts of the Holy Spirit. What the Christians in Samaria had not yet received, then, was this baptism into one body and the gifts of the Holy Spirit.

When Peter and John came to Samaria, they first prayed for the church and then laid hands on them. At this point the Samaritan believers received the baptism of the Spirit, making them one body in Jesus Christ. They also received the gifts of the Spirit, among which may well have been the gift of tongues, so that Simon and others might recognize that the Holy Spirit had been given to them.

Let's be very clear about this point. If someone says, "You

have to have the gift of tongues in order to have the Holy Spirit," I reply that later on, at Antioch of Pisidia, new groups of disciples were filled with the Spirit without any mention of tongues (Acts 13:52). "Well, then, you must have the apostolic ministry!" No, in the very next chapter Paul has hands laid on him by Ananias, a man who is not an apostle, and he receives the Holy Spirit. "Oh, then it must be by the laying on of hands!" Well, in Acts 10, although Peter the Apostle is at the house of Cornelius, the Holy Spirit is given to the hearers *before* he can lay his hands on them (Acts 10:44).

It is apparent from these divergent accounts that the Spirit of God is sovereign, doing things in different ways because that is His sovereign right. If He had come upon these Samaritan disciples when they first believed in Jesus, there could easily have developed a church of the Samaritans which was separate from the church of the Jews. The Jews and the Samaritans had no dealings with each other, so if the Spirit of God had come upon this church when Philip first preached there, two separate churches might well have emerged. So through these apostles who came down from Jerusalem the Spirit of God was saying, "There are not two bodies, but only one. There is one church, and the Samaritans belong to it equally with the Jews."

No Repentance

Now we come to the exposure of Simon's false ministry.

Now when Simon saw that the Spirit was given through the laying on of the apostles' hands, he offered them money, saying, "Give me also this power, that anyone on whom I lay my hands may receive the Holy Spirit" (Acts 8:18,19).

How little Simon understood of the grace, majesty, and might of God! Through the centuries Simon's very name has been attached to the sin of trying to buy religious power with money. This sin is called "simony" because of this man. Notice how bluntly Peter exposes Simon's sin:

But Peter said to him, "Your silver perish with you, because you thought you could obtain the gift of God with money!" (Acts 8:20).

In a literal translation of the Greek Peter actually says, "To hell with you and your money!" It was a terrible thing that this man had suggested—that God's power could be bought with money, as though God were but a mechanism, subject to man's whim and caprice. Then Peter points out the problem to Simon:

You have neither part nor lot in this matter, for your heart is not right before God (Acts 8:21).

Peter sees that Simon's heart is full of bitterness and is enslaved by iniquity. He had never really been set free! So Peter continues,

Repent therefore of this wickedness of yours, and pray to the Lord that, if possible, the intent of your heart may be forgiven you (Acts 8:22).

God reads hearts and does not need to listen to words. But this man was so far from repentance that this is how he replied:

And Simon answered, "Pray for me to the Lord that nothing of what you have said may come upon me" (Acts 8:24).

In other words, Simon refused to take personal action; he wished only to escape the penalty. There is no hint here that he actually repented of his insult against God's grace. It is no wonder that this man ultimately became one of the earliest and greatest opponents of the gospel. In the apocryphal books you can read that Simon Magus hindered the gospel everywhere it went and continued to be the exponent of the Devil's lie. God's grace is able to overpower evil, but as Jesus said, "Woe to him by whom temptations come! It would be better for him if a millstone were hung round his neck and he were cast into the sea than that he should cause one of these little ones to sin" (Luke 17:1,2).

Chapter Fifteen

Have Spirit, Will Travel

Acts 8:25-40

Three symbols present at the beginning of the church were to
characterize the ministry of the Holy Spirit throughout the age of
the church. These three were the mighty rushing wind, the
tongues as of fire, and the proclamation of the truth in various
languages (the gift of tongues). The mighty rushing wind repre-
sents the Spirit in His sovereignty, and this aspect of the Spirit's
work is especially prominent in this part of Acts. Jesus had said,
"The wind blows where it wills, and you hear the sound of it, but
you do not know whence it comes or whither it goes; so it is with
everyone who is born of the Spirit" (John 3:8). The wind is an
apt symbol of the sovereign direction of the Holy Spirit. This
account is a very beautiful picture of this sovereignty. The account opens as Peter and John are on their way back from
Samaria to Jerusalem:

> Now when they had testified and spoken the word of the
> Lord, they returned to Jerusalem, preaching the gospel to
> many villages of the Samaritans (Acts 8:25).

Three words here indicate the normal, usual activity of Christians.
Peter and John came down to Samaria and first of all *testified*—
they shared what they had experienced, what God had done with
them through Jesus Christ. Then they spoke the word of the
Lord—they *prophesied*—by proclaiming truth. Finally, as Peter
and John returned to Jerusalem they *evangelized*—they preached

141

the gospel. These three things—prophesying, testifying, and evangelizing—make up the normal activities of Christian witness. The apostles then proceeded in an orderly way back to Jerusalem, doing the ordinary, expected things—empowered, of course, by the Holy Spirit.

Freedom to Interfere

But in the next verse we have an unusual, extraordinary, unpredictable activity of the Spirit of God:

> But an angel of the Lord said to Philip, "Rise and go toward the south to the road that goes down from Jerusalem to Gaza." This is a desert road. And he rose and went (Acts 8:26,27).

The ministry of angels, according to the Bible, goes on all the time. They are "ministering spirits sent forth to serve, for the sake of those who are to obtain salvation" (Heb. 1:14). All of us, all the time, are being touched and affected by the ministry of angels, but we usually do not see them.

So here is an unexpected agency through which the Holy Spirit works. An angel appears to Philip and gives him an unexplained command to go south on the road to Gaza. He could not have picked an emptier stretch of road. There are no cities or villages en route, but notice the beautiful way in which Philip obeys the angel's command. He just goes. He leaves the awakening that is going on in Samaria, with its demands for training and teaching, and goes down to a desert road.

The point I wish to make is that the experience of Peter and John, as well as that of Philip, are both records of Spirit-filled activity. Peter and John were obeying the Holy Spirit when they testified, prophesied, and evangelized. But Philip was also obeying the Holy Spirit when he was sent by an angel to a desert place. Some people say that you are being led of the Holy Spirit only when you are doing unusual things under unusual circumstances. But this is obviously untrue. The Holy Spirit often leads in the ordinary and the usual, and He can be very effective in this way. Yet we must also leave room for the unpredictable character of God—the sovereign, vital, fresh ministry of the Holy Spirit which moves in ways that nobody can anticipate. We need to give Him the freedom to interfere in our programs.

In the story of Elijah, God showed the prophet that He did not intend to work through the power of the wind, the earthquake, or the fire, as Elijah wanted Him to do. God said instead, "No, I'm going to work through the still, small voice of an awakened conscience. That is what will change the whole land." We must be prepared in our Christian life for this sovereign activity of the Spirit of God which can use both usual and unusual circumstances in our lives.

The Man and the Moment

The rest of the chapter is a wonderful story of the Holy Spirit's adequacy to handle Philip's adventure, and to prepare it all in advance. It begins with a prepared man:

> And he rose and went. And behold, an Ethiopian, a eunuch, a minister of Candace the queen of the Ethiopians, in charge of all her treasure, had come to Jerusalem to worship and was returning; seated in his chariot, he was reading the prophet Isaiah (Acts 8:27, 28).

The eunuch was a prepared man. He had great responsibilities as the secretary of the treasury of Ethiopia. He had great influence throughout all of Ethiopia and Egypt, for he worked with the queen. (Candace was the title given to all the queens of Ethiopia.) He was obviously a searching man. He had come to Jerusalem to worship at the temple, even though he was definitely not a Jew. You cannot read this account without detecting a note of disillusionment. The eunuch is going home, but he is evidently not satisfied. Having bought a copy of the Book of Isaiah, he is reading this scroll aloud as he rides along in his chariot. This is Philip's perfect moment, prepared by the Holy Spirit:

And the Spirit said to Philip, "Go up and join this chariot." So
Philip ran to him and heard him reading Isaiah the prophet,
and asked, "Do you understand what you are doing?" And he
said, "How can I, unless some one guides me?" And he invited
Philip to come up and sit with him. Now the passage of the
scripture which he was reading was this: "As a sheep led to the
slaughter or a lamb before its shearer is dumb, so he opens not
his mouth. In his humiliation justice was denied him. Who can
describe his generation? For his life is taken up from the
earth." And the eunuch said to Philip, "About whom, pray,
does the prophet say this, about himself, or about someone
else?" (Acts 8:29-34).

This whole situation is a tremendous manifestation of the prepa-
ration and timing of the Holy Spirit. As Philip is walking along
the road, a chariot comes over the hill. At the precise moment
when the man in the chariot passes the evangelist he happens to
be reading aloud from Isaiah 53, the great passage that predicts
the coming of the Messiah, the suffering Savior. What exquisite
timing!

Notice how the Spirit is guiding the conversation. Philip says
to him, "Do you understand what you are reading?" And the
man replies, "How can I, unless some one guides me?" This
answer indicates the eunuch's awareness that it takes God's full
provision to make Scripture clear through teachers that He raises
up. Charles Spurgeon, the great English preacher, used to say, "I
never could understand why some men set such great value on
what the Holy Spirit says to them, and so little value on what He
says to anyone else." Some people seem to think that only what
God says to *them* counts—as though He were not speaking to
anyone else. But God has provided both the Scriptures and
teachers. It takes both to enter into the full knowledge of truth.

Beginning with this Scripture

So the eunuch invites Philip to come up and sit with him. He
was at the right passage but was puzzled by it, as many have been

puzzled since. For this is the passage that deals with the sufferings of Jesus. Most of the Old Testament passages depict the Messiah as coming in triumph and power and glory, riding over the enemies of Israel as the great King, the One who would restore peace to the earth, who would break in pieces all the weapons of war and cause the people to beat their swords into plowshares and their spears into pruning hooks.

But these pictures of a suffering Savior have always been a puzzle to some readers, especially the Jews. And they puzzled the eunuch also. "Why does the prophet say that the Messiah has to die? Or is he speaking of the Messiah at all? Is he perhaps speaking of himself?" Philip, who knew the Scriptures, was ready with the answer:

> Then Philip opened his mouth, and, beginning with this scripture, he told him the goods news of Jesus. And as they went along the road they came to some water, and the eunuch said, "See, here is water! What is to prevent my being baptized?" And he commanded the chariot to stop, and they both went down into the water, Philip and the eunuch, and he baptized him (Acts 8:35-38).

Philip began with the Scripture that the eunuch was reading, and he undoubtedly pointed out some of the predictions in this passage:

> But he was wounded for our transgressions, he was bruised for our iniquities; upon him was the chastisement that made us whole, and with his stripes we are healed. All we like sheep have gone astray; we have turned everyone to his own way; and the Lord has laid on him the iniquity of us all (Isa. 53:5,6).

What a marvelous place from which to preach the gospel! What good news that the coming of Jesus Christ has solved the problem of man's guilt! How this man must have rejoiced to hear the story of Jesus, and of how this passage was fulfilled in Him.

But evidently Philip went on from there, obeying the Great Commission:

> Go therefore and make disciples of all nations, baptizing them
> in the name of the Father and of the Son and of the Holy
> Spirit, teaching them to observe all that I have commanded
> you (Matt. 28:19, 20).

Philip must have told the eunuch what baptism means, how it is a
symbol of the life that has been received from Jesus Christ, and
that by being baptized an individual is saying, "I have asked Jesus
to enter my life and to be my Lord. I have received a new life in
Him." So when they came to a place where there was some water
at the side of the road (again at the precise timing of the Holy
Spirit), the eunuch said, "See, here is water! What hinders me
from being baptized?" So they went down and Philip baptized
him.

Caught Up in Joy

The closing passage is full of wonderful things:

> And when they came up out of the water, the Spirit of the
> Lord caught up Philip; and the eunuch saw him no more, and
> went on his way rejoicing. But Philip was found at Azotus,
> and, passing on, he preached the gospel to all the towns till he
> came to Caesarea (Acts 8:39,40).

This sounds like a miracle, doesn't it? It sounds as if Philip
suddenly disappeared, and the eunuch, looking around with
amazement, couldn't find him, so he finally went on his way.
Although it can be read this way, I think that Philip and the
eunuch came up from the water, the two were so carried away
with the excitement and tremendous joy of the moment that
they did not realize they had gone their separate ways. As the
eunuch came up from the water he was so overwhelmed with the
joy of finding Jesus that he didn't even notice that Philip failed to
get back into the chariot with him. He went on his way rejoicing,
and it was some time before he thought of Philip again.

Philip, on the other hand, was so caught up with what God

had done, with this glorious gem of an experience that God had given him, that he didn't realize for awhile that the eunuch had driven off and left him there. He was so lost in his thoughts as he went along that it was some time before he came to himself. When he did, he found that he was at Azotus, on the coast road. There he began to preach systematically in the towns all the way up the coast to Caesarea.

Hasn't this happened to you? It has to me. I've gotten to thinking about some dramatic work of God's as I have been driving along in my car, and suddenly I've found myself in an entirely different town than the one for which I had set out.

This is the adventure of the Spirit-filled life. Yet when Philip got to Azotus he didn't wait for another dramatic leading like this. He began where he was and started preaching right up the coast until he came to Caesarea. The Spirit-filled life will have much that is routine, much that is usual, much that is ordinary, but that "ordinary" is all touched with the flame of heaven. And there will also be these wonderful moments when out-of-the-ordinary, amazing things will suddenly begin to develop, and you become aware that you are being carried along into events which dovetail together in a way that only a divine hand could have planned. It is then that you realize that God is at work in an amazing way. This is the truly normal Christian life.

Chapter Sixteen

Beloved Enemy

Acts 9:1-19

During the time that the gospel was being systematically preached throughout every village of Samaria and Judea by outstanding leaders such as Philip and others, the Lord was also doing something else. He was preparing the human instrument by which the gospel would move into the third stage, even today unfinished, of reaching the uttermost parts of the earth. We now come to the conversion of the Apostle Paul.

Young Saul of Tarsus, the enemy, the persecutor, the relentless pursuer of Christians, is now to be arrested by Jesus Christ and conscripted to bear the gospel to the uttermost parts of the earth. No story shows more beautifully the relentless, loving pursuit of God than the story of Saul. Here, in the opening words of Acts 9, we find a man pursued:

> But Saul, still breathing threats and murder against the disciples of the Lord, went to the high priest and asked him for letters to the synagogues at Damascus, so that if he found any belonging to the Way, men or women, he might bring them bound to Jerusalem (Acts 9:1,2).

Notice three interesting things in this passage. First, Saul was breathing threats and murder. In the King James Version it says that he was "breathing out threats and slaughter," but the literal

Greek says that he was "breathing in threats and murder," for this was the very atmosphere and climate in which Saul lived and breathed. Later, in his appearance before King Agrippa, Saul himself tells the king how he had felt at this time:

> I myself was convinced that I ought to do many things in opposing the name of Jesus of Nazareth. And I did so in Jerusalem; I not only shut up many of the saints in prison, by authority from the chief priests, but when they were put to death I cast my vote against them. And I punished them often in all the synagogues and tried to make them blaspheme; and in raging fury against them I persecuted them even to foreign cities (Acts 26:9-11).

Obviously Saul was a man motivated, a man empowered by guilt. He never forgot the death of Stephen. To quiet his conscience he engaged in this terrible pursuit of the church.

The name given to the Christians in this passage is most interesting. They are referred to as "belonging to the Way." Names like this are invariably given by opponents. A group may take a name for themselves, but the name that sticks is usually the one that others call them. Other people saw that these Christians had a different life-style. They were characterized not by self-centeredness but by love and acceptance and understanding and tolerance. There was something about them that reminded them of Jesus, who was Himself "the Way, the Truth, and the Life." So they dubbed His followers "those belonging to the Way."

Beyond the Border

The third significant thing in this paragraph is that it was not until Saul was outside the borders of his homeland—brought there by the Lord Jesus—that he was converted. This was because Saul was scheduled to become the mighty apostle to the Gentiles. Until this time the gospel had gone out only within the bounds of

Israel. But now, in calling the man who is to carry it further, God takes Saul out of his land to convert him. This is the wonderfully graphic symbolism by which God underlines His truth.

In the next section we have the story of how the hands of Jesus closed in on the soul of Saul of Tarsus:

> Now as he journeyed he approached Damascus, and suddenly a light from heaven flashed about him. And he fell to the ground and heard a voice saying to him, "Saul, Saul, why do you persecute me?" And he said, "Who are you, Lord?" And he said, "I am Jesus, whom you are persecuting; but rise and enter the city, and you will be told what you are to do." The men who were traveling with him stood speechless, hearing the voice but seeing no one. Saul arose from the ground; and when his eyes were opened, he could see nothing; so they led him by the hand and brought him into Damascus. And for three days he was without sight, and neither ate nor drank (Acts 9:3-9).

Although there have been many scholarly attempts to explain what happened here on a purely natural level, Paul himself is utterly consistent throughout his whole life as to just what he heard and saw on this occasion. He says he saw the Lord Jesus. Paul based his claim to apostleship upon the fact that he had seen Jesus Christ. He heard His voice and he knew what it said, and what it said had great effect on him. This was not a lightning stroke or an epileptic seizure, as has been suggested; this was the appearance of Jesus Christ to the man who was to be the mighty apostle to the Gentiles.

Exposure and Development

The first words that Jesus speaks to Saul are very significant. He says to him, "Saul, *why* are you persecuting Me?" What are your reasons? What do you hope to accomplish? I'm sure that in the hours of darkness that followed, young Saul debated this question many, many times. Why? What was it that had driven him like this? What was it that led to such violent activity against the program of God? In answering this question Saul would come to a great understanding of himself and of human life.

Next, Jesus says, "Arise and enter the city, and there you will be told what to do." This indicated a tremendous reversal of Saul's whole approach to life. He is now experiencing for the first time the life-style which belongs to a Christian. Conversion is a revolutionary change of government, resulting in a radical change in behavior. That is what happened to Paul. No longer would he be giving the orders; no longer would he be directing men and sending them where he wanted them to go in order to do what he wanted them to do; now he would be told what he was to do.

It has always seemed to me that in the conversion of Saul there is a striking parallel to the process of photography. At this moment God printed a picture of Jesus Christ upon the soul of this young man. From that moment on, anyone who looked at Paul the Apostle never saw Paul; he saw Jesus Christ. The fundamental principle of photography is to take light-sensitive salts. spread them on a film, and then keep them in total darkness until the precise moment when what you want recorded is exposed to it.

Saul was a young man who was very sensitive to the things of God, but he was kept in darkness until this moment of exposure. In that blinding light the image of Jesus Christ was printed indelibly on his soul. After exposure to light, film is always kept in darkness to develop while it is placed into dark and bitter waters for awhile. Here the newest apostle was led by the hand into the city of Damascus, where for three days and nights he neither ate nor drank, while the image to which he was exposed was developed and imbedded unforgettably in his heart. Saul of Tarsus was crucified, and Jesus Christ was seen in his life from then on.

Strength from the Body

Now we see the Lord Jesus moving further to reclaim this man from the worthlessness of his empty life and to set him on the path of true value:

> Now there was a disciple at Damascus named Ananias. The Lord said to him in a vision, "Ananias." And he said, "Here I am, Lord." And the Lord said to him, "Rise and go to the street called Straight, and inquire in the house of Judas for a man of Tarsus named Saul; for behold, he is praying, and he has seen a man named Ananias come in and lay his hands on him so that he might regain his sight." But Ananias answered, "Lord, I have heard from many about this man, how much evil he has done to thy saints at Jerusalem; and here he has authority from the chief priests to bind all who call upon thy name." But the Lord said to him, "Go, for he is a chosen instrument of mine . . ." (Acts 9:10-15).

What is the first thing Paul experienced as a Christian? The life of the body of Christ. Two unknown, obscure Christians are sent to him, and he is immediately helped by the strengthening that can come from the body. First there is a man named Judas—that is all we know about him—to whose house Saul was led. While he is there a man named Ananias is sent to minister to him.

There is a joyful, poetic irony in the Holy Spirit's choice of two names which elsewhere in the New Testament are tainted: Judas and Ananias. Judas Iscariot was the betrayer of our Lord, and Ananias was the first Christian to manifest the deceit and hypocrisy of an unreal life. Yet here two people who bear these same two names are honored and used of God.

Ananias was understandably reluctant to come to the man who had been ready to drag people off to prison and put them to death because they were Christians. Yet Saul of Tarsus begins to experience the joy of body life through these other Christians ministering to him.

Gentiles First

After Paul is called he is given a specific ministry:

But the Lord said to him [Ananias], "Go, for he is a chosen

instrument of mine to carry my name before the Gentiles and kings and the sons of Israel; for I will show him how much he must suffer for the sake of my name" (Acts 9:15,16).

Paul was told two things about his ministry: first, where it would be manifested. It was to be to three groups. His primary obligation was to go to the Gentiles, the non-Jewish nations of the world. Later he would call himself the Apostle to the Gentiles.

His second area of ministry was to kings. He was to penetrate the power structures of his day, to speak to those at the top, to minister to those who were in positions of authority and influence. Throughout the Book of Acts you will find the record of Paul's repeated appearances before governors, procurators, kings, and finally even the Emperor himself.

Last on the list, Paul was to minister to the sons of Israel. Paul always wanted to put this first. He longed to be the instrument by which Israel would be redeemed. But Paul wasn't running the program anymore; God was. Though Paul had great impact on his own nation, the sons of Israel, he was primarily the minister to the Gentiles.

Then the Lord revealed how Paul was to make his impact. "I will show him," God said, "how much he must suffer for my name's sake." Paul was called to suffer. This is a word we don't like—suffer. Yet the Christian life invariably involves suffering. Why is that? Why is suffering a part of the normal Christian life? Because suffering is the activity of love. It is love that bears hurt. It is love that takes the blame, that takes the hurt, that is willing to endure. Anyone who is called to be a Christian must learn to love, must learn to suffer. Love is always hurt in the process of loving. That is why, in this fallen world, love must always suffer.

The man Paul was called to enter into the sufferings of Jesus Christ because Jesus loves fallen men and wants to redeem them. But he cannot redeem them without being hurt in return. So Paul as Jesus' servant was also called to be hurt. What a tremendously responsive instrument he became! How much he suffered in order that he might manifest the love of the heart of God for a lost and wicked world!

When we are called to follow Jesus Christ we are calle

suffer. We have to forgive, and that hurts, doesn't it? We don't like to forgive; we would rather hold a grudge and take vengeance. We want our ego to be fed and our pride to be satisfied. But God has called us to suffer and forgive.

Filled and Enlightened

Paul is not called to do this in his own strength, but in the power of the Spirit.

So Ananias departed and entered the house. And laying his hands on him he said, "Brother Saul, the Lord Jesus, who appeared to you on the road by which you came, has sent me that you may regain your sight and be filled with the Holy Spirit." And immediately something like scales fell from his eyes and he regained his sight. Then he rose and was baptized, and took food and was strengthened (Acts 9:17-19).

No one can manifest the suffering of Christian love without being filled with the Holy Spirit. As Ananias laid his hands on Paul he was filled with the Holy Spirit. There were no tongues, no sign, no manifestation; there was simply a quiet infilling of the Holy Spirit, just as occurs today with anyone who believes in Jesus Christ.

The filling immediately changed Paul's vision; scales fell from his eyes. I think this is both literal and symbolic. All those long, built-up prejudices of a Pharisee against Gentiles; all the bigotry, pride, and prejudice that twisted and distorted his view of the Gentile world—all this disappeared in a moment. This man saw the whole world, Jews and Gentiles alike, as men and women bearing the image of God and needing to be redeemed. As Paul later tells us in his own words, he learned to judge no man according to the flesh, but to see in him only a potential subject for the kingdom of God.

Then Paul was baptized. He took his place as a Christian. He identified himself with those who bear the name of Jesus Christ.

God has now prepared his instrument to carry the gospel to all the nations of the world. Those of us who are not Jews owe a great debt to Paul; without him we would not have believed and come to know our Lord Jesus. Paul's life and ministry has made a great impact upon every one of us.

Chapter Seventeen

The Yoke of Christ

Acts 9:19-31

Paul became a Christian on the road to Damascus, but he didn't start living the Christian life in all its fullness and power until a number of years later. He had many lessons to learn first. The simple fact of Saul's conversion did not by itself account for the mighty influence which this man had throughout the rest of his life. Jesus had said to His disciples, "Come to me, all who labor and are heavy laden, and I will give you rest." Then he added, "Take my yoke upon you, and learn from me, for I am gentle and lowly in heart, and you will find rest for your souls" (Matt. 11:28,29). These two verses indicate two separate stages in Christian development—two stages which Paul experienced, as does every believer who wishes to walk in the footsteps of the Lord.

The simplest possible statement of the gospel is the three words of Jesus: "Come unto me." He does not add any qualifications; just come as you are. That is His invitation, and he promises, "I will give you rest." Millions of people through the centuries have come to Christ on these terms and found that He gives exactly what He says He will—rest of heart.

But then Jesus says something more: "Take my yoke upon you, and learn from me . . . and you will find rest for your souls." You become a Christian by coming to Christ, but you cannot really live the Christian life until you assume the yoke of Christ.

A yoke is a shaped piece of wood by which two draft animals are tied together to pull a load. To take on the yoke of Christ means to submit to Him, to His leadership, to His Lordship. And to do this is to discover what it means to live as a Christian is really intended to live.

Because He Is Lord

Paul had to learn this. There was a definite period during which Paul was being taught how to take the yoke of Christ upon himself. That is what we will see in this account, as a new paragraph begins:

> For several days he was with the disciples at Damascus. And in the synagogues immediately he proclaimed Jesus, saying, "He is the Son of God." And all who heard him were amazed, and said, "Is not this the man who made havoc in Jerusalem of those who called on this name? And he has come here for this purpose, to bring them bound before the chief priests" (Acts 9:19-21).

These verses describe the initial witness of the Apostle after he became a Christian. He came into Damascus and stayed there, blind, for three days and nights. Then Ananias came and prayed for him. Paul received his sight, was filled with the Holy Spirit, and was baptized; he had all the basic equipment necessary for living the Christian life.

Then Paul immediately began to proclaim Jesus, saying, "He is the Son of God." In other words, Paul started proclaiming the lordship of Jesus Christ, that He is the Lord of heaven and earth. This is fundamental to the new birth. You become a Christian when you understand and accept in your own life the *authority and lordship* of Jesus. The idea that you become a Christian when you accept Him as your Savior is not in the New Testament. You will find no verses in the New Testament which offer the Lord Jesus as the Savior of the world; He is offered as Lord. When He is accepted as Lord, He becomes Savior.

We have twisted this around and, unfortunately, millions of people have tried to accept the saviorhood of Jesus without His lordship. As a result there is no change in their lives. It is understanding the fact that Jesus is the Son of God, that Jesus is Lord, which produces the change of heart that allows the Holy Spirit to bring a person fully into the family of God. Remember that this mighty Apostle, in writing to the Romans, says, "if you confess with your lips that Jesus is Lord and believe in your heart that God raised him from the dead [that he is a risen Lord, a living Lord], you will be saved" (Rom. 10:9). That is when salvation occurs.

Into the Desert

The next verse immediately notes a different kind of testimony by the Apostle:

> But Saul increased all the more in strength, and confounded the Jews who lived in Damascus by proving that Jesus was the Christ [the Messiah] (Acts 9:22).

Paul proved from the Scriptures that Jesus is the Messiah. But he didn't do this at first. Luke is giving us a condensed survey of what happened in the early church, and he leaves out certain events which we need to fill in from other Scriptures. We learn from the Epistle to the Galatians that a period of many days—three years, in fact—comes between verses 21 and 22. What happened during this time? In Paul's own account of his conversion he says,

> But when he who had set me apart before I was born, and had called me through his grace, was pleased to reveal his Son to me, in order that I might preach him among the Gentiles, I did not confer with flesh and blood, nor did I go up to Jerusalem to those who were apostles before me, but I went away into Arabia; and again I returned to Damascus (Gal. 1:15-17).

Luke tells us that immediately after the Apostle was converted he began to tell everybody that Jesus is Lord. But after a few days he found it necessary to somehow square this with all he had been taught in the Scriptures. And so, taking the Scriptures under his arm, he went away into the desert.

As he began to read through the Old Testament again, he saw Jesus Christ on every page. Everywhere he turned, the Old Testament was speaking of Jesus. In the Prophets, in the Psalms, in Moses and the Law—everywhere it pointed to Jesus. Paul began to discover that the sacrifices and offerings were all pictures of Jesus. The very configuration of the Tabernacle was a picture of the life of Jesus. Jesus was everywhere throughout the Old Testament.

Paul's Plan

As Paul studied, a great yearning and conviction grew in his heart. He did what many of us have done; he tried to second-guess what God was doing and what his part would be. He was still a young man. He had his whole life to live before him. So he tried to figure why it was that Christ had arrested him in such dramatic fashion on the Damascus road. He came up with this conviction (the Bible does not say this explicitly, but it is clearly implied in several places): God had determined that Paul would be the person to reach the nation of Israel. This stubborn, obstinate nation of the Jews needed someone who would convince them beyond a shadow of doubt that Jesus was the Messiah.

Paul himself tells us in certain places in his Epistles that there was a great, eager hunger in his heart to reach his own people. In Romans he says, "I could wish that I myself were accursed and cut off from Christ for the sake of my brethren, my kinsmen by race" (Rom. 9:3). He hungers to reach them, and he thinks he sees what God is doing. He reasons, "I've got all the equipment, all the background, all the training, all the ability necessary to reach this stubborn people."

So he came back to Damascus from Arabia confident, knowledgeable, eager, and able in the Scriptures, and he increased all the more in strength in confounding the Jews by proving from the Scriptures that Jesus is the Christ. Imagine what Paul must have felt like. Here he is a seminary graduate with a D.D. degree (Doctor of the Desert), feeling called to go into Damascus to wipe out all the opposition before him and to convince these stubborn Jews that Jesus is their Messiah. And he does this. He is unbeatable in debate. He proves from the Scriptures that Jesus is the Christ.

His Greatest Moment

Paul wins all the battles but loses the war. He wins all the arguments, but he never wins a soul. In spite of his tremendous dedication, in spite of the skillful and knowledgeable arguments he employs, in spite of the untiring, sincere effort of this dedicated, zealous young man, the Jews remain locked in stubborn and obstinate unbelief. In fact, the situation gets much worse. We read,

> When many days had passed, the Jews plotted to kill him, but their plot became known to Saul. They were watching the gates day and night, to kill him; but his disciples took him by night and let him down over the wall, lowering him in a basket (Acts 9:23-25).

What humiliation! Paul was going to show the world how much he could do for this new Master he had found. But instead he finds himself humiliated and rejected. His own friends finally have to let him down over a wall by night. He walks away into the darkness in utter, abject failure and defeat.

The amazing thing is, and it really is amazing, that many years later as Paul writes to the Corinthians he recounts this episode: "The greatest event in my life was when they took me at night and let me down over the wall of Damascus in a basket. That was the most meaningful experience I have ever had since the day I met Christ" (2 Cor. 11:30-33).

Why was this so? Because then and there the Apostle began to learn the truth which he tells us about in his Letter to the Philippians: "Whatever gain I had, I counted as loss . . . because of the surpassing worth of knowing Christ Jesus my Lord" (Phil. 3:7,8). That is, "The night they let me down over the wall in a basket, I began to learn something. It took me a long time to catch on, but there I began to learn that God didn't need my abilities; He needed only my availability. He just needed me—not my background or my ancestry. He didn't even need my knowledge of Hebrew. In fact, God didn't have any particular intention of using these things to reach the Jews; He was going to send me to the Gentiles." Though Paul didn't fully understand it at the time, it was at this point that he began to assume the yoke of Christ and to enter the school of the Spirit.

Jesus Himself tells us what the curriculum of this school is: "Learn of me, for I am meek and lowly in heart." Ambition and pride must die. If you are depending on yourself, God evaluates all you do as worth nothing. This is what Paul began to learn, and through this experience his pride began to die. Yet it died hard, and we find him still struggling:

And when he had come to Jerusalem he attempted to join the disciples; and they were all afraid of him, for they did not believe that he was a disciple. But Barnabas took him, and brought him to the apostles, and declared to them how on the road he had seen the Lord, who spoke to him, and how at Damascus he had preached boldly in the name of Jesus. So he went in and out among them in Jerusalem, preaching boldly in the name of the Lord. And he spoke and disputed against the Hellenists; but they were seeking to kill him (Acts 9:26-29).

Here Paul comes to Jerusalem still aflame, determined to show the world how much he can do for Christ. Yet at first even the disciples would have nothing to do with him. But after Barnabas swore that Paul was indeed a disciple, and that he had been preaching in the name of Jesus, the other disciples listened to him.

Get Out of Town

From Galatians we learn that Paul's stay in Jerusalem was only fifteen days. But in this short time this zealous young Christian bigot went into the synagogues and began to argue and dispute, again to prove that Jesus was the Christ. It had the same effect as in Damascus: they tried to kill him. And another incident occurred which is not recorded in this part of Acts, but is found later in Paul's account of this same period:

> When I had returned to Jerusalem [from Damascus] and was praying in the temple, I fell into a trance and saw him [Jesus] saying to me, "Make haste and get quickly out of Jerusalem, because they will not accept your testimony about me" (Acts 22:17,18).

Here the Lord appears to Paul and says, "You don't belong here in Jerusalem. I don't want you to be the apostle to Israel; I want you to be the apostle to the Gentiles. Get out of this city. Nobody is going to listen to you here." Notice how Paul argues with Jesus:

> And I said, "Lord, they themselves know that in every synagogue I imprisoned and beat those who believed in thee. And when the blood of Stephen thy witness was shed, I also was standing by and approving, and keeping the garments of those who killed him" (Acts 22:19,20).

"Why, Lord," Paul says, "you don't seem to realize who I am. I'm the one who was persecuting the church with great eagerness and malice; these Jews know how vigorously I opposed the church. And now that I know that those whom I persecuted were right, the Jews will have to listen to me, Lord. You're throwing away your greatest opportunity here! They can't help but believe when they hear it from me!" But listen to what the Lord replied:

> And he said to me, "Depart; for I will send you far away to the Gentiles" (Acts 22:21).

"I have a different program for you, Paul. All you need is Me. Until you learn that, you will never be of any value to Me at all. So I want you to leave town."

Back in Acts 9 we read,

And when the brethren knew it, they brought him down to Caesarea, and sent him off to Tarsus (Acts 9:30).

Then notice this beautiful last verse:

So the church throughout all Judea and Galilee and Samaria had peace and was built up; and, walking in the fear of the Lord and in the comfort of the Holy Spirit, it was multiplied (Acts 9:31).

It might seem strange that Luke would add here that the church had peace as soon as they got rid of Paul. But now that we understand what is really happening here, from correlating these other Scriptures, it makes perfect sense.

So the believers sent Paul to Tarsus—the hardest place on earth to learn anything, and yet the best place to be, for it was Paul's home. For a period of from seven to ten years nothing is heard of the Apostle Paul. He is home, learning the essential lesson that God is trying to teach all of us—that all God needs is you and me the way we are, available to do whatever *He* wants to do through us. The life of an eager, zealous Christian who is trying to serve God in the flesh is not a Christian life at all. It is false Christianity, and it turns people away from Christ.

Remember how Peter tried to put his zeal into action, how in the Garden of Gethsemane he drew his sword and slashed away. All he did was chop off the ear of the high priest's servant. And that is all *we* do when we try to serve God in the energy of the flesh—we go around chopping off peoples' ears! If it weren't for the healing grace of the Lord Jesus, who picks up all those severed ears and puts them back in place, nobody would ever speak to us again!

Finally, after seven to ten years at home, the Spirit of God leads Barnabas to go down to Tarsus to find Paul and bring him to Antioch, where there has been a spiritual awakening. Paul comes back chastened and broken—and available. And then begins that mighty career in the power of the Holy Spirit, that unparalleled manifestation of the life of Jesus Christ that changed the whole Roman Empire and the course of history. Paul had learned the essential lesson, "Apart from me you can do nothing" (John 15:5), so he says, "I have been crucified with Christ; it is no longer I who live, but Christ who lives in me; and the life I now live in the flesh, I live by faith in the Son of God, who loved me and gave himself for me" (Gal. 2:20). It was on these terms that Paul shook the world for Christ.

Chapter Eighteen

Three Faces of Death

Acts 9:32-10:23

Death takes many forms. We begin to die long before we actually take our last breath; death seizes us in many areas of our life other than the physical. Boredom is death. Despair is also death. Fear and worry are forms of death. Mental illness is death, and so is bitterness of spirit. Death can rule over great areas of our lives long before we ever die; we know this from experience. But the great Good News of Jesus Christ is that He has come to abolish death, whatever form it may take.

The Apostle Peter, like all true Christians, was a channel of the power of Jesus Christ as he traveled around among the churches of Judea and Samaria. Christ's power accomplished one great thing through Peter everywhere he went: it abolished death. In the three incidents of this passage we will see how in each case the power of Jesus Christ abolished death. The first incident is a picture of death's power to paralyze:

> Now as Peter went here and there among them all, he came down also to the saints that lived at Lydda. There he found a man named Aeneas, who had been bedridden for eight years and was paralyzed. And Peter said to him, "Aeneas, Jesus Christ heals you; rise and make your bed." And immediately he rose. And all the residents of Lydda and Sharon saw him, and they turned to the Lord (Acts 9:32-35).

The airport outside Tel Aviv is at the ancient town of Lydda, now known as Lod. It was to this village that Peter came on his way down from Jerusalem, as he visited the new churches of Judea and Samaria that had sprung up in all the villages. In Lydda he finds a man who had been paralyzed for eight years. Peter says to him, "Jesus Christ heals you; rise and make your bed."

Here we have a paralysis of the body. For eight years it had held this man impotent, unable to fulfill God's intention for human life. But that can happen to the spirit as well. When it does, you experience a paralysis of the will. Perhaps there are things you have been wanting to do, knowing that you ought to do them. But you never have, because you are looking to your own resources; you are expecting some new sensation or feeling to motivate you to get moving. It is to that kind of condition that this story makes its appeal. Jesus Christ says to you, "Rise and begin to live. Do what you ought to do, in My name. Stand up and be strong, in My name. Rise and be well."

Interrupted Service

The next incident is even more remarkable, for here we find death in its most fearful form, the actual ending of life:

> Now there was at Joppa a disciple named Tabitha, which means Dorcas or Gazelle. She was full of good works and acts of charity. In those days she fell sick and died; and when they had washed her, they laid her in an upper room. Since Lydda was near Joppa, the disciples, hearing that Peter was there, sent two men to him entreating him, "Please come to us without delay" (Acts 9:36-38).

Death's power to interrupt service is pictured for us in this account. The outstanding characteristic of this woman was grace and selfless love. She helped others. Her very name meant Gazelle, an animal characterized by grace and charm. Suddenly, unexpectedly, her service was brought to an end. She fell sick as the power of the enemy struck hard and viciously, and she was laid low and died. But now comes the sequel:

So Peter rose and went with them. And when he had come,
they took him to the upper room. All the widows stood beside
him weeping, and showing coats and garments which Dorcas
made while she was with them. But Peter put them all outside
and knelt down and prayed; then, turning to the body, he said,
"Tabitha, rise." And she opened her eyes, and when she saw
Peter she sat up. And he gave her his hand and lifted her up.
Then, calling the saints and widows, he presented her alive.
And it became known throughout all Joppa, and many believed in the Lord. And he stayed in Joppa for many days with
one Simon, a tanner (Acts 9:39-43).

This is a marvelous miracle—a restoration from the dead. Here is a
woman whose ministry of love and selflessness was interrupted by
death. But now, by the hand of God and the power of Jesus
Christ, she is restored to her ministry of good works.

Of course Dorcas later died again, because this incident is
primarily a picture intended to teach us that this kind of death
can happen to the human spirit, too. Something can interrupt the
progress of a spiritual life which is beginning to flourish and bear
fruit. Some circumstance, some event or experience, can interrupt
it and cause it to die. The person loses his zeal and becomes cold,
hard, and indifferent—bitter of spirit. He is literally like someone
dead.

This kind of death can go on for years. Edwin Markham the
great Christian poet, once entrusted a banker with the settlement
of an estate. The banker betrayed him, and Markham lost all his
money and was rendered penniless. It made him bitter, and for
several years he could write no poetry. Then one day as he was
trying to write, Markham sat at his desk aimlessly scrawling
circles. As he doodled the thought suddenly struck him of the
great circle of God's love, and of how it takes us in. He was struck
with inspiration and wrote these words:

> I drew a circle and shut him out;
> Heretic, rebel, a thing to flout.
> But Love and I had the wit to win;
> We drew a circle that took him in.

Markham forgave the banker and was able to resume his ministry.

After that came some of his greatest poems. That is what Jesus Christ can do. He can heal the bitterness that may be in your life, rendering you cold and indifferent to the needs of others.

Cornelius and the Angel

The third incident is most significant, for it concerns a healing in the spirit of the Apostle Peter himself. It begins with another man who is living 27 miles up the coast from Joppa, in the Roman garrison headquarters at Caesarea:

> At Caesarea there was a man named Cornelius, a centurion of what was known as the Italian Cohort, a devout man who feared God with all his household, gave alms liberally to the people, and prayed constantly to God. About the ninth hour of the day he saw clearly in a vision an angel of God coming in and saying to him, "Cornelius." And he stared at him in terror, and said, "What is it, Lord?" And he said to him, "Your prayers and your alms have ascended as a memorial before God. And now send men to Joppa, and bring one Simon who is called Peter; he is lodging with Simon, a tanner, whose house is by the seaside." When the angel who spoke to him had departed, he called two of his servants and a devout soldier from among those that waited on him, and, having related everything to them, he sent them to Joppa (Acts 10:1-8).

Here is a picture of a moral, upright, and generous man—but one who is not yet born again. The gift of God, eternal life in Jesus Christ, is what this man needs, and God is moving to answer that need.

The great question which I am asked more frequently than any other, especially by non-Christians, is, "What about the man who lives up to the light he has, and is faithful to what he knows, but has never heard of Jesus Christ? What happens to him?" The story of Cornelius shows us what happens to a man like that. When he is obedient to the light he has, God will take it upon Himself to give him more light and to lead him to the place where he can come to know Jesus Christ. This is in line with what we read in Hebrews: "Without faith it is impossible to please [God]." It goes on to say, "For whoever would draw near to God . . ." must have two qualifications—just two: he must believe that God exists, and he must believe that God rewards those who seek Him (Heb. 11:6). He must believe that God will meet his quest by giving him more light along the way.

That was Cornelius' situation. He believed that God existed. He was tired of all the emptiness and sensuality that was connected with Roman paganism. He was seeking God; he knew that God would help him. He was praying, asking God to help him—and God does help. Notice that God doesn't send an angel to preach the gospel to Cornelius; angels are not commissioned to preach the gospel. God sends an angel to tell him where he can find a *man* who will preach the gospel, who will tell him the truth about Jesus Christ.

When the angel appears, Cornelius is very frightened, as we would also be. But the angel tells him to send to Joppa for a man named Peter, who is living in the house of Simon, a tanner. That was about as good an address as you could ask for, since tanners prepare hides, and it is a smelly occupation. Once the messengers arrived in Joppa, they merely needed to follow their noses in order to find Peter!

The Death of Prejudice

In the meantime God was working at the other end to prepare the meeting of these men:

> The next day, as they were on their journey and coming near the city, Peter went up on the housetop to pray about the sixth hour. And he became hungry and desired something to eat; but while they were preparing it, he fell into a trance and saw the heaven opened, and something descending, like a great sheet, let down by four corners upon the earth. In it were all kinds of animals and reptiles and birds of the air. And there came a voice to him, "Rise, Peter; kill and eat." But Peter said, "No, Lord; for I have never eaten anything that is common or

unclean." And the voice came to him again, a second time,
"What God has cleansed, you must not call common." This
happened three times, and the thing was taken up at once to
heaven (Acts 10:9-16).

What a strange experience! Why did this happen to Peter? The
answer is that God wanted to heal the death in Peter's spirit—the
death of prejudice, of bigotry and snobbishness. Here is an
apostle who is born again and filled with the Holy Spirit, but who
has a great area of bigotry present in his life.

Choice, Not Exclusion

The Old Testament tells us that God separated the Jews from
the rest of mankind. He did so not on the basis of their superior-
ity, but because He wanted them to demonstrate to all the other
nations of the world the relationship which God wants to have
with mankind. Only in that sense were the Jews the chosen
people.

But in typically human fashion, as we ourselves probably
would have done, the Jews distorted that calling of God, that
pattern of the Old Testament. They began to believe that God
was not interested in Gentiles, but that He only liked Jews. This
has given rise to anti-Semitism by the Gentiles, many of whom
are saying, in that shortest of all poems,

> How odd
> Of God
> To choose
> The Jews!

And so Peter grew up with the attitude that God did not like
Gentiles. Gentiles were a sort of animal, not quite human. They
were not even to be spoken to, let alone to be invited into your
home. A good Jew, as Peter had been taught, would have nothing
to do with a Gentile. If he even touched one accidentally on the
street he would go home and wash. This bigotry was deeply

embedded in the Apostle's heart. He had always thought that God's choice of the Jews also involved His exclusion of the Gentiles.

God cures Peter by revealing the truth in graphic form. He sends a vision of a sheet full of animals which Peter had been taught were unclean. But God's command is, "Rise, Peter; kill and eat." Peter begins at once to argue with the Lord. He says, in the King James Version, "Not so, Lord; for I have never eaten anything that is common or unclean." Obviously you cannot be consistent and say, "Not so, *Lord*." If you say "Lord" then you must not say, "Not so." And if you say "Not so" then He is not Lord!

Notice also the marks of legalism here. Peter says, "Lord, I have never eaten anything common or unclean." That is the language of legalism: "I have *never done* anything like that in all my life." A legalistic spirit is proud of the negative, proud of "never having done" a particular thing. Of course, as a Christian led of the Spirit there are things we won't do—things that are harmful, and which God has forbidden for our own protection. But what is wrong here is being *proud* of the things we won't do. So God rebukes Peter for his legalism. God says to him immediately, "How dare you call unclean what God has called clean!"

Sometimes we call *ourselves* unclean. People have said to me, "I just can't forgive myself. The things I've done are so bad that even though I know God has forgiven me, I can't accept myself." It often helps if we can see that by this attitude we are calling God a liar. We are calling unclean what God has called clean.

We read that this vision appeared to Peter three times. That may be because three is the stamp of the Trinity. God is saying by this threefold occurrence, "Look, all of us—Father, Son, and Holy Spirit—agree that we don't like this bigotry. This is against the Spirit of God—this whole business of prejudice because of color or background or past or deeds or circumstances or whatever." Even the mighty Apostle Peter had to be taught this lesson, not by the *filling* of the Holy Spirit but by the *teaching* of the Holy Spirit.

Setting Aside All Malice

While my daughter was at Wheaton College she wrote to me about a touching incident. At chapel one day, the president of Wheaton College got up and shared with the entire student body a dilemma that he was facing. Many supporters of the school were withholding funds because they were bothered by the many long-haired youths they had seen on their visits. The president said the school was in a serious financial bind because of this; their whole operation was being threatened. And the student body sat there, breathlessly anxious to learn what the administration's stand would be.

Then the president called out of the audience the young man who had the longest hair and beard in the whole student body, and asked him to come up to the platform. Turning to him, he said, "You have long hair, and you have a long beard. You represent the very thing that these supporters of the school are against. I want you to know that the administration of this school does not feel as they do. We accept you, and we love you. We believe that you are here to seek and to find the truth as it is in Jesus Christ." And he reached out and embraced him! The student body rose as one man in a moment of acclaim for their president, for his expression of that kind of love and acceptance.

That is what God wants. The great lesson that God taught the Apostle Peter on this occasion was that these Gentiles were to be his friends and were to be accepted by him.

Now Peter takes the first step toward this goal:

Now while Peter was inwardly perplexed as to what the vision which he had seen might mean, behold, the men that were sent by Cornelius, having made inquiry for Simon's house, stood before the gate and called out to ask whether Simon who was called Peter was lodging there. And while Peter was pondering the vision the Spirit said to him, "Behold, three men are looking for you. Rise and go down, and accompany them without hesitation; for I have sent them." And Peter went down to the men and said, "I am the one you are looking for; what is the reason for your coming?" And they said, "Cornelius, a centurion, an upright and God-fearing man, who is well spoken of by the whole Jewish nation, was directed by a holy angel to send for you to come to his house, and to hear what you have to say." So he called them in to be his guests (Acts 10:17-23).

Ah, the barriers are crumbling; the walls are breaking down! Peter invites these Gentiles in to be his guests. That is the first step. He had never done anything like this before. But that is the language of liberty. Legalism says, "I have never"; liberty in Christ says, "I have never done anything like this *before*." So Peter begins to open up, to accept and take these men in. In this story we can see clearly the character of the grace of God—that He desires to remove all prejudice from the human heart and to make us see each other as we really are—members together of one race, all equally in need of God's redeeming grace in Jesus Christ.

Chapter Nineteen

Peter and Cornelius

Acts 10:23-11:18

It is often suggested that the Book of Acts ought to be called the Acts of the Holy Spirit. I agree. Nowhere is the sovereign superintendency of the Holy Spirit more in evidence than in this wonderful account of how He moved to open the door of faith to the Gentiles. The Spirit's first step was to prepare the heart of a Gentile man, Cornelius, to receive the message of life. He did this by awakening in Cornelius a sense of hunger which he expressed in prayers, in the giving of alms, and in seeking after God. Next the Spirit gave Peter the vision of the sheet let down from heaven with various kinds of animals, birds, and reptiles in it, and He told Peter pointedly that all of them were clean, thus removing the iceberg of prejudice in Peter's heart. Then He brought Peter and Cornelius together. We resume the account as Peter and his accompanying brothers in Christ leave the city of Joppa:

> The next day he rose and went off with them, and some of the brethren from Joppa accompanied him. And on the following day they entered Caesarea. Cornelius was expecting them and had called together his kinsmen and close friends. When Peter entered, Cornelius met him and fell down at his feet and worshiped him. But Peter lifted him up, saying, "Stand up; I too am a man." And as he talked with him, he went in and found many persons gathered; and he said to them, "You

yourselves know how unlawful it is for a Jew to associate with or to visit anyone of another nation; but God has shown me that I should not call any man common or unclean. So when I was sent for, I came without objection. I ask then why you sent for me" (Acts 10:23-29).

Certain human reactions which Luke has recorded for us mark this incident as the authentic account of a real episode. When Peter entered Cornelius' house, this proud Roman centurion fell down at his feet and worshiped Him. It is remarkable that a member of the subjugating military garrison should fall at the feet of one of the subject people and worship him! But so hungry was the heart of Cornelius, so anxious was he to find God, that he was actually willing to worship a Jew.

Prepared for the Gospel

Peter, of course, is embarrassed. He lifts Cornelius up and says, "I'm just a man like you; don't worship me." Peter refuses to accept the homage of this man, which is most interesting in view of the Roman Catholic claim that Peter was the first Pope. Also, Peter is obviously still uneasy at entering the home of a Gentile, as we see from his explanation. As they go into the house he says to Cornelius, "You know how unlawful it is for a Jew to associate with or to visit anyone of another nation." Now this was not God's law; it was man's law. But Peter had been taught a lesson, and though he obviously doesn't fully understand it yet, he says "God has shown me that I should not call any man common or unclean, and so I've come. What do you want of me?" Cornelius now tells his side of the story:

And Cornelius said, "Four days ago, about this hour, I was keeping the ninth hour of prayer in my house; and behold, a man stood before me in bright apparel, saying, 'Cornelius, your prayer has been heard and your alms have been remembered before God. Send therefore to Joppa and ask for Simon who is called Peter; he is lodging in the house of Simon, a tanner, by the seaside.' So I sent to you at once, and you have been kind enough to come. Now therefore we are all here present in the sight of God, to hear all that you have been commanded by the Lord" (Acts 10:30-33).

This was one of the most strategic home Bible classes ever held. In a home Bible class a man opens his home, gathers his friends, has some refreshments ready, and invites a teacher to come and present the gospel to his friends. It is a most workable format, as it was on this occasion when Cornelius gathered his kinsmen and friends together. They are waiting expectantly now for the word of the gospel.

Now we come to Peter's message—the purpose for which the Holy Spirit has maneuvered these men together. Here is the great message that will set Cornelius free:

> And Peter opened his mouth and said, "Truly I perceive that God shows no partiality, but in every nation anyone who fears him and does what is right is acceptable to him" (Acts 10: 34,35).

Here we have the first formal preaching of the gospel—the first preaching of Jesus—to a Gentile audience. Peter makes seven distinct points, and they comprise a marvelous unfolding of the Good News. The first point is that God shows no partiality. He receives anyone, anywhere, from any background or race, any social class, any station in life. It doesn't make any difference to Him.

Do not misread what Peter says. The words "in every nation anyone who fears him and does what is right is acceptable to him" mean that God recognizes that such a man has an honest heart and a correctly receptive attitude. But Cornelius was still unregenerate, without Christ. He still had no life within his heart. Yet he was acceptable to God because he was honest. Anyone, in any circumstance, who comes to God with an honest heart will find an open door to the truth about Jesus Christ. That is the first part of the gospel.

Man as God Intended

Then Peter goes on to make the second point:

You know the word which he sent to Israel, preaching good news of peace by Jesus Christ (he is Lord of all), the word which was proclaimed throughout all Judea, beginning from Galilee after the baptism which John preached: how God anointed Jesus of Nazareth with the Holy Spirit and with power . . . (Acts 10:36-38).

Immediately Peter moves to the first coming of Christ, to the incarnation. Notice how he puts it in human terms. Jesus came as a Man through whom God worked in love and power. He did not come primarily to display His deity, to show us how God behaves; He came to show us how man behaves as God intended him to be—indwelt by God. That is what it takes to be a man.

The third point of Peter's message goes on from there:

. . . how he [Jesus] went about doing good and healing all that were oppressed by the devil, for God was with him. And we are witnesses to all that he did both in the country of the Jews and in Jerusalem (Acts 10:38,39).

The next great feature of the Good News is that when Jesus Christ arrived He destroyed the effects of evil everywhere He went. He did this openly, before witnesses, where everyone could see. Everywhere Jesus went He set people free and brought once more to human hearts the hope that there is a way out of the desperate bondage of fallen humanity.

I will never forget the experience of a young man who came into our congregation a few years ago. He was not accustomed to attending church—he had not been raised in a church at all—but his heart was hungry. He came, not knowing what the people would be like. He felt that Christians were super-snobbish and self-righteous—people who felt they were better than others. As I was speaking, I read these verses:

Do you not know that the unrighteous will not inherit the

kingdom of God? Do not be deceived; neither the immoral, nor idolaters, nor adulterers, nor homosexuals, nor thieves, nor the greedy, nor drunkards, nor revilers, nor robbers will inherit the kingdom of God. And such were some of you (1 Cor. 6:9-11).

For some reason that morning I stopped at that point and said, "How many in this congregation belong in this category? How many of you have ever been guilty of some of these things?" All over the congregation hands began to rise. This young man took a look around, saw the forest of hands, and said to himself, "These are my kind of people."

Such were some of you, set free. That is what Christ does. "He went about doing good and healing all that were oppressed by the devil" as a demonstration of what God is accomplishing in the work of redemption.

Peter's fourth point is sobering, and very briefly stated:

They put him to death by hanging him on a tree . . . (Acts 10:39).

It is almost as though he does not want to dwell on it. All he says is, "They put him to death. . . ." Jesus was killed by the most shameful means possible. Even the Romans recognized that. Cicero, the Roman orator, said, "The cross is so terrible that it should not be mentioned in polite company." Yet by this means Jesus, the Man who went about doing good, was put to death. Peter passes quickly to the fifth point:

. . . but God raised him on the third day and made him manifest; not to all the people, but to us who were chosen by God as witnesses, who ate and drank with him after he rose from the dead (Acts 10:40,41).

This is impressive, isn't it? Peter said, "I was one of those witnesses who saw Jesus after He rose from the dead. It was no hallucination, because we ate and drank with Him after He rose from the dead. Only bodies can eat and drink, and there He was." God's power was greater than man's, and He broke the barriers of death.

Every Man Must Choose

Peter then makes the sixth point:

And he commanded us to preach to the people, and to testify that he is the one ordained by God to be judge of the living and the dead (Acts 10:42).

In other words, says Peter, Jesus commanded us to preach Him as a living person. He is not dead; He is alive and available to all men everywhere. Not only that, but He is the ultimate crisis of all men. Jesus stands at the end of every path down which men go, and He waits there as the One ordained by God to be the Judge of the living and the dead.

Finally Peter reaches the seventh point and the glorious climax to it all:

To him all the prophets bear witness, that everyone who believes in him receives forgiveness of sins through his name (Acts 10:43).

Peter says, "You Romans may not appreciate this fully, but everything that Jesus did was predicted by the prophets long before He ever came, all that He would be like and all that He would do was written down. Every prophet bore witness to this one fact: the only way you can ever find forgiveness of sins is by believing in Him."

We are guilty people, and we know it. That is why we are so restless, why we often cannot stand to be alone with ourselves. Our oppression because of our sense of guilt is overwhelming. So the prime need of our lives is to be forgiven, to have nothing in the past to worry about, to have nothing which makes us uncertain of the future and nothing which makes us unwilling to appear before God. Through Jesus Christ our sins are forgiven. All the future ones, as well as those of the past, are forgiven in Jesus Christ.

God, therefore, has no quarrel with you; He loves you, He accepts you. Whatever you do, He will continue to love you and accept you. If you have been born again you know that this is the greatest and most unending blessing of your life—to wake up every morning and remember that you stand as a beloved child in God's presence. You are His, and for that reason He will be with you in every circumstance, all day long.

Holy Interruption

Peter had more to say, but right at this point a most dramatic interruption occurred:

> While Peter was still saying this, the Holy Spirit fell on all who heard the word. And the believers from among the circumcised who came with Peter were amazed, because the gift of the Holy Spirit had been poured out even on the Gentiles. For they heard them speaking in tongues and extolling God. Then Peter declared, "Can anyone forbid water for baptizing these people who have received the Holy Spirit just as we have?" And he commanded them to be baptized in the name of Jesus Christ. Then they asked him to remain for some days (Acts 10:44-48).

The Holy Spirit interrupted Peter, just as He had on the Day of Pentecost, and what He did here is very significant. Peter had just given these people something to believe, the death and resurrection of Jesus. Then he told them, "The prophets bear witness that everyone who believes in Jesus receives forgiveness of sins." As soon as Peter's audience heard these words they believed. And immediately upon believing they received the Holy Spirit, just as Jesus said they would. He had said,

> If anyone thirst, let him come to me and drink. . . ."Out of his heart shall flow rivers of living water." Now this he said about the Spirit, which those who believed in him were to receive . . . (John 7:37-39).

As soon as they heard, they believed, and when they believed, they received. The Holy Spirit refused to wait until the altar call!

As on the Day of Pentecost, the gift of tongues was the sign of the coming of the Holy Spirit, indicating to Peter and these other Jews that the Gentiles were being received on the same basis as the Jews had been. Peter got the point. He said, "Can anyone forbid water for baptizing these people who have received the Holy Spirit just as we have?" Notice that the baptism of the Holy Spirit does not do away with the baptism of water. One is a symbol of the other. These men were baptized with water *because* they had been baptized with the Spirit.

An End to the Matter

The last part of the story shows us what happens when truth encounters deep-seated prejudice and tradition:

> Now the apostles and the brethren who were in Judea heard that the Gentiles also had received the word of God. So when Peter went up to Jerusalem, the circumcision party criticized him, saying, "Why did you go to uncircumcised men and eat with them?" But Peter began and explained to them in order: "I was in the city of Joppa praying; and in a trance I saw a vision, something descending, like a great sheet, let down from heaven by four corners; and it came down to me. Looking at it closely, I observed animals and beasts of prey and reptiles and birds of the air. And I heard a voice saying to me, 'Rise, Peter; kill and eat.' But I said, 'No, Lord: for nothing common or unclean has ever entered my mouth.' But the voice answered a second time from heaven, 'What God has cleansed you must not call common.' This happened three times, and all was drawn up again into heaven.
>
> "At that very moment three men arrived at the house in which we were, sent to me from Caesarea. And the Spirit told me to go with them without hesitation. These six brethren also accompanied me, and we entered the man's house. And he told us how he had seen the angel standing in his house and saying, 'Send to Joppa and bring Simon called Peter; he will declare to you a message by which you will be saved, you and all your household.'
>
> "As I began to speak, the Holy Spirit fell on them just as on us

at the beginning. And I remembered the word of the Lord, how he said, 'John baptized with water, but you shall be baptized with the Holy Spirit.' If then God gave the same gift to them as he gave to us when we believed in the Lord Jesus Christ, who was I that I could withstand God?" When they heard this they were silenced. And they glorified God, saying, "Then to the Gentiles also God has granted repentance unto life" (Acts 11:1-18).

That is the way to answer arguments. Just tell what God has done. Recount the actions of God. When these men saw how God had acted, there was nothing further they could say. And so they ceased arguing and instead praised God, glorifying Him for extending life outward to all men.

Chapter Twenty

Recognition of a Church

Acts 11:19-30

Animated discussion has been stimulated over the question of when the gospel was first brought to the Gentiles. Did the first breakthrough take place at the meeting of Philip and the Ethiopian eunuch, in Acts 8, or was it when Peter came to the house of Cornelius, in Acts 10? The following two verses in Acts 11 provide a clear answer to the question:

> Now those who were scattered because of the persecution that arose over Stephen travelled as far as Phoenicia and Cyprus and Antioch, speaking the word to none except Jews. But there were some of them, men of Cyprus and Cyrene, who on coming to Antioch spoke to the Greeks also, preaching the Lord Jesus (Acts 11:19,20).

It was at the time of the persecution that broke out over Stephen, described in Acts 7, that the gospel began to penetrate the Gentile world. In other words, it was almost from the very beginning of the church. The wonderful thing about this gospel message is that it was carried by obscure, unknown men and women—Jews who had been converted to Christianity. Some were Hebrew-speaking Jews who preached only to the Jews, and others were Greek-speaking Jews, men of Cyprus and Cyrene on the north coast of Africa. When they came to Antioch they began to preach to the Greek-speaking Gentiles there. This soon led to a natural consequence, the beginning of a new church:

And the hand of the Lord was with them, and a great number that believed turned to the Lord. News of this came to the ears of the church in Jerusalem, and they sent Barnabas to Antioch. When he came and saw the grace of God, he was glad; and he exhorted them all to remain faithful to the Lord with steadfast purpose; for he was a good man, full of the Holy Spirit and of faith. And a large company was added to the Lord (Acts 11:21-24).

The result of this first preaching was that a great many Gentile converts came to Christ. But the disciples at Jerusalem never thought that God would move to reach the Gentile world, so they hardly knew what to make of it. Were these people real Christians? Was it possible that Gentiles could actually come to Christ just as a Jew could?

Gentle Investigator

To settle the issue, the disciples sent Barnabas to Antioch. What a great choice they made! Great-hearted Barnabas didn't try to control this new thrust by the Holy Spirit; he simply came down to investigate it, to see what God had been doing. Barnabas was a Greek-speaking Jew, having come from Cyprus himself, so he could identify with the Christians from Cyprus and Cyrene who did the preaching here.

Antioch was a strategic city, the third-largest in the Roman Empire. It was noted as a sports center—chariot races were a specialty—and as a place of culture. Also, about five miles outside the city, in the temple of Daphne, sex was enthroned and worshiped through priestesses who were really religious prostitutes. Yet this new church had arisen in the midst of the city's corruption, and Barnabas was sent to discover what was going on.

Barnabas is characterized as a good man, full of the Spirit and full of faith. He was a good man—an easygoing, cheerful, open-hearted, gracious individual—and full of the Holy Spirit. This, of course, is the supreme qualification. In other words, Barnabas was a man to whom the wisdom, understanding, and love of God were continuously being imparted. Being full of the Holy Spirit meant that the fruits of the Spirit were evident in his life: love, joy, longsuffering, patience, and gentleness, because he was drawing upon the power of an indwelling Holy Spirit.

Expecting God to Work

Being a man of faith, Barnabas acted upon what God said. He didn't wait for his feelings. A man of faith simply believes God and expects Him to act. He doesn't even think about how he feels. Many people think that unless they have a tremendous sense of expectation or excitement within them, they have no faith. But faith is not a feeling. Rather, it is simply believing that God will do what He has promised, and then acting on that basis.

When Barnabas came to Antioch he expected to be led of God, that God would give him the wisdom to handle whatever developed. So it was no surprise to him that things began to work out immediately. When Barnabas arrived he found a group of men and women who were undoubtedly Christians—which is what he had been sent to discover. "When he came and saw the grace of God, he was glad." What did he see that convinced him that these men and women were genuine? Luke says that Barnabas saw the grace of God. Now how do you see grace? Grace means the goodness of God poured out into a life—an invisible quality. How do you see that?

The word for grace here is the same word that the Apostle Paul employs in speaking about the gifts of the Holy Spirit:

But grace was given to each of us according to the measure of Christ's gift (Eph. 4:7).

In other words, grace is a gift of the Spirit, such as love, wisdom, knowledge, faith, discernment, prophecy, teaching, and so forth. When Barnabas saw the gifts of the Holy Spirit at work he knew that these people were real Christians. In Hebrews 2 we are told that the gospel was first declared by the Lord, was then preached by those who knew Him, and was finally confirmed by signs and wonders and *by the distribution of the gifts of the Holy Spirit* (Heb. 2:3,4).

To a Young Church

Barnabas saw also that these people comprised a church, for they shared together the common life of Jesus Christ. And since they were a church, this is the basis on which Barnabas spoke to them. He gave them a message designed for a new church, with two important points. He exhorted them first to remain faithful to the Lord, He said, "In receiving the Lord, you have received all there is; there is nothing more for Him to give you. It's true that you haven't yet laid hold of it all, but through the years you will develop what you have. But there is nothing more to be added." As Peter puts it, "His divine power *has granted to us* all things that pertain to life and godliness" (2 Pet. 1:3). So Barnabas says, "Remain faithful to what you have. Don't go after anything else. You don't need anything new. In the Holy Spirit you have all that God will give you."

But, second, do it intelligently and with purpose. "Remain faithful to the Lord with steadfast purpose." The Greek here means "according to a set plan." They were to remember that they needed to learn more of the Lord through His Word. Already they had the Old Testament Scriptures, which were full of Christ. And the New Testament Scriptures were gradually beginning to come into being. They were to begin understanding what God was doing in Jesus Christ. They were to seek, and read, and study, because the Scriptures reveal Christ.

Don't Look Down

So Barnabas exhorted these new believers to work intelligently at learning about Jesus, through reading the Scriptures, seeking His face, and learning to pray all through the day in every situation. New Christians need to learn this more than anything else, and many make a fatal mistake at this point. At first they have their faces fixed on Jesus, and it is wonderful. They sense immediately the joy that fills their hearts as they come to know this glorious, living Lord. But gradually their focus shifts. Instead of seeing Jesus they begin to look at themselves. They start feeling of their feelings. And when they do that, they are like Peter walking on the water, who began to sink when he took his eyes off Jesus and put them on his circumstances. Many young Christians fail to concentrate on the Lord Himself, to find joy in Him and to glory in His presence. In becoming occupied simply with the things the Lord *does* for them, they lose the sense of His presence and fail to seek His face. That is why they sink and often disappear from Christian fellowship for awhile.

The immediate result of Barnabas' exhortation was that a large company was added to the Lord. When you get people looking to the Lord and not to themselves, you will find that people are added to the Lord. And this is the way the church increases; the true means of adding to the church is to add *people to the Lord.* If they belong to the Lord, they already belong to the church.

The phrase "a large company" leads to the next new thing that happened in Antioch:

So Barnabas went to Tarsus to look for Saul (Acts 11:25).

The word "so" means "because of this large company." There were so many new people to teach, and such an overwhelming number of new converts had come in, that Barnabas went to Tarsus to look for Saul:

And when he had found him, he brought him to Antioch. For a whole year they met with the church, and taught a large company of people . . . (Acts 11:25,26).

In the ten years since Barnabas last saw him, Paul had not been entirely idle, as he tells us in Galatians. He preached the Word throughout the regions of Syria and Cilicia, the area around Tarsus. Probably many of the visions and revelations from the Lord which Paul mentions in several places occurred during this time. But he had learned one great secret—that only his depen-

dence upon Jesus at work in him made him an effective worker
for Jesus Christ. When Paul had learned this lesson, the Lord sent
Barnabas over to Tarsus to find him, to bring him to Antioch,
ready to begin his great worldwide ministry.

In connection with this, we learn of another first:

> . . . and in Antioch the disciples were for the first time called
> Christians (Acts 11:26).

It is clear from this brief statement that it was not the disciples
who named themselves Christians, but the people of Antioch. The
word means "those belonging to Christ" or "Christ's men." As
these Christians talked about Jesus to men everywhere—Jesus the
Christ, the Messiah—the Gentiles around them labeled them
"Christ's men." (You can tell from this that they didn't talk
about the church; they talked about Jesus!)

Although the people of Antioch used the term contemptuous-
ly, the disciples thought it was wonderful to be called Christ's
men, so they adopted the name and called themselves Christians.
The people of Antioch, in a sense, called them "Jesus freaks,"
and the disciples agreed. In current usage, to be a freak is to be
deeply committed to something. So when these believers were
heard witnessing about Jesus, they were called Jesus freaks. But
they were not in the least offended. They counted it a joy to
suffer reproach for His name's sake, so committed were they to
the cause of Jesus Christ.

Plenty Meets Need

The last scene in this chapter brings to our attention another
first-time ministry:

> Now in these days prophets came down from Jerusalem to
> Antioch. And one of them, named Agabus, stood up and
> foretold by the Spirit that there would be a great famine over
> all the world; and this took place in the days of Claudius. And
> the disciples determined, every one according to his ability, to

send relief to the brethren who lived in Judea; and they d l so, sending it to the elders by the hand of Barnabas and Saul (Acts 11:27-30).

Unfortunately, both the word "prophecy" and the gift of prophecy have become associated only with the ability to predict the future. But the word primarily means "to cause to shine." Prophecy is the ability to *illuminate* the Word of God—to make it shine. These prophets who came from Jerusalem were men who illuminated the darkness in people's lives with the truth of God. Occasionally, as in this case, they were also able to illuminate the future.

On this specific occasion one of the prophets predicted that there would soon be a great famine throughout the world, and this came true just a few months later. Not only does Josephus, the Jewish historian, record this famine, but two Roman historians, Suetonius and Tacitus, both mention the great famine in the days of Claudius. We can positively date this event at A.D. 44 and 45. And we know that it was especially severe in Judea.

But the most important fact is that when these disciples heard from the Spirit that there was going to be a great famine, they believed Him and began to prepare for it. The whole account is a beautiful picture of the concern of the body. They didn't wait for heartrending appeals from the brethren in Judea: "We don't have anything to eat, and we don't have any clothes to wear." The Christians anticipated the need in response to the Holy Spirit, and they had the gift all ready when the effects of the famine struck. They sent the gift by their favorite teachers, Barnabas and Saul (Paul), who had been teaching there in the church for a year.

What wonderful instruction in the Holy Spirit this church must have had under the leadership of these two men! How clearly they understood the essential nature of the church—that it is a body in which one member shares life with another. Notice that there is no sense of hierarchy here, no priesthood. There is no super-spiritual class of saints called the clergy. There is just the body of Christians together, one group in Jerusalem and another in Antioch. One has need and the other has plenty, so the body in

Antioch sends to the body in Jerusalem the things required to meet their need and to share together in the life that is in Jesus Christ.

The essential characteristics of a church are all here: the gifts of the Spirit, the shared life in Jesus, the proclamation of the word, the teaching of Scripture, the sharing of the body. Every now and then, when men drift away from this pattern, the Holy Spirit breaks out afresh and starts it all over again. Right now we are living in one of those times. God is again renewing the church in our own time. How we ought to rejoice in that great fact!

Chapter Twenty-One

Let Us Pray

Acts 12:1-25

A moment ago we saw how the young church was being blessed as God's Spirit was moving in the city of Antioch to enlarge the Christian enterprise and to thrust the gospel out to the Gentiles. That great city was being shaken by the presence of the Christians in its midst. But now, coming back to Jerusalem, we discover that the enemy strikes a slashing blow in retaliation against the church there. We may be twenty centuries away from these events, but we are not twenty centuries away from the Book of Acts, because this is the account of the work of the timeless Spirit of God. He is the same in every age, working today just as He did here in the Book of Acts.

So far we have seen the body of Christ at work. Now let's look at three events which Luke puts together—events which at first seem somewhat unrelated. But no event in the Word of God is ever without significance, so let's try to see why Luke, guided by the Holy Spirit, has chosen these particular events for our instruction. The three events are the murder of the Apostle James, the deliverance of Peter from prison by the intervention of an angel, and the death of Herod the King. First is the murder of James:

> About that time Herod the king laid violent hands upon some who belonged to the church. He killed James the brother of John with the sword; and when he saw that it pleased the

Jews, he proceeded to arrest Peter also. This was during the
days of Unleavened Bread (Acts 12:1-3).

This means that the murder and arrest took place during the
Passover season, the same period of the year when Jesus Himself
was taken and crucified. But now the year is A.D. 44. We can
date it very precisely because the date of Herod's death, also
recorded here, is well-known in ancient history. So these events
occurred about twelve years after the crucifixion and resurrection
of Jesus and the coming of the Spirit on the Day of Pentecost.
The church had been growing and expanding during these twelve
years, but now the enemy strikes hard by moving Herod the King
to seize James the brother of John and to behead him with the
sword. (This Herod is not the one before whom Jesus appeared.
This is his brother, known as Herod Agrippa, the father of the
Herod before whom Paul will later appear.)

This account indicates that James was an important leader in
the church, although his name has not been mentioned previously
in the Book of Acts. James's brother was John. How often James
and John appear together in the Gospel accounts! These were the
brothers whom Jesus very affectionately called "sons of thunder"
because of their swashbuckling dispositions. They were filled with
zeal, and it is interesting to watch how the Lord worked with
these two young men. John He particularly loved and drew close
to Himself. But both were strong in Jesus' affections.

It was these two boys who came to Jesus with their mother,
asking to be granted positions at the right and left hand of the
throne of glory when Jesus came into His kingdom. Jesus answered their request with a question: "Are you able to drink the
cup that I am to drink?" By this He meant His violent death on
the Cross. And with typical teenage enthusiasm and ardor they
said, "Yes, we're able!" Jesus told them, "You will drink my cup,
but to sit at my right hand and at my left is not mine to grant,
but it is for those for whom it has been prepared by my Father"
(Matt. 20:22,23). In the words "You will drink my cup" Jesus
indicated that these men would die violent deaths. James was the
first of the apostles so to die, and John was the last. So the deaths

of these brothers form a parenthesis within which all the apostles lived and labored and eventually died.

No Automatic Deliverance

The church is evidently not too disturbed when James is taken captive. Undoubtedly they think that God will release him from prison, perhaps by sending an angel, as He had done before. But imagine the shattering effect upon them when James is beheaded—actually executed—and the sad news comes to the waiting church. The church is stunned, and when Peter is arrested there is great concern:

> And when he [Herod] had seized him [Peter], he put him in prison, and delivered him to four squads of soldiers to guard him, intending after the Passover to bring him out to the people. So Peter was kept in prison; but earnest prayer for him was made to God by the church (Acts 12:4,5).

No more fun and games now; the church is very serious. They realize that they cannot count upon the automatic deliverance of God. And so earnest prayer is made on behalf of Peter. You can see that Herod is afraid of something too, because he takes special care to see that Peter is held securely. He details four squads—sixteen soldiers altogether—to watch this one man. Peter is under the guard of four soldiers at all times—two chained to his wrists and two standing guard at the door of his cell. But Peter is not afraid, for we read:

> The very night when Herod was about to bring him out, Peter was sleeping between two soldiers, bound with two chains, and sentries before the door were guarding the prison; and behold, an angel of the Lord appeared, and a light shone in the cell; and he struck Peter on the side and woke him, saying, "Get up quickly." And the chains fell off his hands. And the angel said to him, "Dress yourself and put on your sandals." And he did so. And he said to him, "Wrap your mantle around you and follow me." And he went out and followed him; he did not

know that what was done by the angel was real, but thought he was seeing a vision. When they had passed the first and the second guard, they came to the iron gate leading into the city. It opened to them of its own accord, and they went out and passed on through one street; and immediately the angel left him. And Peter came to himself, and said, "Now I am sure that the Lord has sent his angel and rescued me from the hand of Herod and from all that the Jewish people were expecting" (Acts 12:6-11).

What a remarkable story! I think Peter really expected to be executed, but he slept nevertheless, obviously trusting that God would glorify Himself either by his death or by delivering him so that he could live. Yet when the angel comes, Peter is taken by surprise.

Seeing is Not Believing

As we read this account we can see what a supernatural deliverance this was. The angel takes no note of the guards whatsoever, but simply strikes the chains from Peter's arms. The guards were evidently either confused or asleep. And notice how bewildered Peter is. The angel has to tell him, "Now get up. Put on your shoes. Wrap your mantle around you." He leads him by the hand out into the city streets. Peter is not sure what's happening, but when he gets outside and sees the iron gate open of its own accord, he knows that God is at work. And the realization suddenly strikes him that God has indeed set him free from prison.

Then we get this interesting and most human account of what happens when Peter comes to the church:

When he realized this, he went to the house of Mary, the mother of John, whose other name was Mark, where many were gathered together and were praying. And when he knocked at the door of the gateway, a maid named Rhoda came to answer. Recognizing Peter's voice, in her joy she did not open the gate, but ran in and told that Peter was standing at the gate. They said to her, "You are mad." But she insisted that it was so. They said, "It is his angel!" But Peter continued knocking; and when they opened, they saw him and were amazed. But motioning to them with his hand to be silent, he described to them how the Lord had brought him out of the prison. And he said, "Tell this to James and to the brethren." Then he departed and went to another place (Acts 12:12-17).

Nothing is more humorous than this picture of Peter, valiantly pounding away at the door, while the girl is inside, having forgotten to let him in, trying to explain to thse Christians that God has answered their prayers. But they don't believe her. At first they think she is insane, but finally she persuades them to come out—and then they see Peter, still banging away. At this point they believe, but are amazed that God has answered their prayers!

The account closes with the story of the cruelty of Herod:

Now when day came, there was no small stir among the soldiers over what had become of Peter. And when Herod had sought for him and could not find him, he examined the sentries and ordered that they should be put to death. Then he went down from Judea to Caesarea and remained there (Acts 12:18,19).

Four innocent soldiers die because of this man's stubborn unbelief. He will not believe that God has acted. As the soldiers tell their tale, the only explanation he will accept is that these men had betrayed their trust and had somehow connived with Peter's friends to release him. So he orders their deaths. Then he goes down to his headquarters in Caesarea, on the coast. Here's the final story of what happened to Herod:

Now Herod was angry with the people of Tyre and Sidon; and they came to him in a body, and having persuaded Blastus, the king's chamberlain, they asked for peace, because their country depended on the king's country for food. On an appointed day Herod put on his royal robes, took his seat upon the throne, and made an oration to them. And the people shouted, "The voice of a god, and not of man!" Immediately an angel

of the Lord smote him, because he did not give God the glory;
and he was eaten by worms and died.

But the word of God grew and multiplied. And Barnabas
and Saul returned from Jerusalem when they had fulfilled
their mission, bringing with them John, whose other name was
Mark (Acts 12:20-25).

Josephus, the Jewish historian, also records the death of Herod.
He describes this occasion when Herod met with the people of
Tyre and Sidon in what we now call Lebanon. These people were
dependent upon Judea, and especially upon Galilee, for food.

So when the king came out, dressed in his royal robes, they
flattered him. When he spoke to them they cried out, "Why, this
is a voice of a god, and not a man!" And this pompous, vain king
believed them. It's almost incredible to imagine the tragic, twisted
mentality of a man like this, a man who could actually believe
that he had so much power that he had become a god. Luke tells
us that Herod was immediately stricken by an angel of the Lord,
and that he was eaten of worms and died. I don't know what
Luke's exact diagnosis is here (perhaps it was a stroke), but some
sudden catastrophe befell Herod and, as Josephus tells us, within
two or three days he died.

What does this mean? This was God's way of demonstrating
the ultimate folly of the idea that we have what it takes to
produce all that life requires, and that we do not need anyone or
anything else—especially God. But God would remind us that our
very life, our very breath—all that we have and are—come from
Him, and that we are fools to think that we have some power of
our own, apart from Him, on which to operate.

As we review the events of this chapter there are some ques-
tions that come to mind. Why did Luke choose to put these three
events together in this account? And, of course, the preeminent
question is, "Why was James killed and Peter delivered? Couldn't
God have saved James as well?" Well, why didn't He? The only
answer that this chapter suggests is found in verse 5, the key to
the chapter:

So Peter was kept in prison; but earnest prayer for him was made to God by the church (Acts 12:5).

The prayer made the difference. Peter was kept in prison, as was James. The difference lay in the word *but*. ("But" is always a crisis word. It indicates a change in direction.) "But earnest prayer to God was made for Peter by the church," and as a result Peter was free. Perhaps you're thinking, "If God determined that James would die and Peter would be set free, what difference did the prayer of the church make?"

Called to Participate

Let us never forget what James (not this James, but Jesus' brother, who wrote the Epistle of James) says: "You do not have because you do not ask" (Jas. 4:2). In His wisdom God has arranged for His people to participate in the things He does. He is impressing upon His people here in Acts that when danger threatens the program of God or the people of God, it is a call to prayer. Prayer becomes a mighty, powerful thrust on the part of the people of God to change events. Basically, prayer is the most natural and normal response of a heart that is dependent on God. The basic *motive* of prayer is a sense of dependence. If you really think that God, and God alone, can work, and that there are elements of a situation which only *He* can change—then you pray. This is what happened to the early church. When they realized that James had been put to death, and that this vicious attack of the enemy could be successful, it suddenly crystalized in their minds that they had a part to play in God's program. They were to go to God in earnest prayer that Peter might be delivered. And God set him free in a wonderful way.

God works in the same way today as He did in those first-century days, and He will respond to our prayers in very much the same way. This doesn't mean that everything we pray for will be granted. Sometimes God overrules our prayers. But prayer does other things as well, even when the things for which we pray are *not* granted.

Releasing God's Mercy

First of all, prayer has the ability to postpone or delay the judgment of God—or the victory of Satan, as in this case. James was killed, but Peter's execution was postponed to a later day. Prayer may not remove the threat entirely, but it can change the time schedule. That is the consistent teaching of the Scriptures about prayer.

We are facing the imminent occurrence of the events predicted in the Bible for the last days. But there have been times in the past when the world has approached the edge of the precipice of the last days. Threatening personalities have appeared whom many people have mistakenly identified as the Antichrist. Yet each time, because of the grave dangers present, God's people woke up and began to cry out to Him. A spiritual awakening followed, and the world moved back from the brink of destruction.

Today we are perhaps further over the edge toward the ultimate disaster than we have ever been before. But once again God's people are waking up, crying out to Him. This is the only hope in our day—that once more God will turn the clock back a bit, delay the schedule, bring us back from the brink, and allow perhaps another generation to grow up in relative peace and liberty in order to know the glory of the gospel in its delivering power. It is my conviction that, in order for God to allow the events of the last days to finally happen, He must remove His church from the earth. In order to take the salt out of society He will remove the church and thus allow the final display of man's evil and enmity to come to full fruition in the last days. But prayer can delay it.

A second thought about the prayers of the church is the clear implication that Peter was at peace even though he was in prison. How could he sleep on the night of his execution? If you knew that you were to be executed tomorrow morning—that your head was to be chopped off—would you have a good night's sleep tonight? Peter slept peacefully. But it was not that he was such a great man of faith—Peter was like us, often weak and fearful—it was because the church was praying for him. That is why God gave him peace of heart. Prayer does this for us when we undergo times of difficulty and trouble.

Third, notice that prayer can produce sudden changes, like the death of Herod. I don't think the church was praying for the king to die. We are not told in Scripture to pray in this way about those in authority. But the church was praying that God would intervene, and as a result of their intercession God was "free" to act in unusual and remarkable ways. This vicious, cruel tyrant, to whom human life meant nothing, was suddenly removed from the scene because of a people who were responsive to God and dependent upon Him, and who cried out to Him for His help.

In Mysterious Ways

This is what Paul means when he says that we often do not know how to pray as we ought to in complicated and intricate situations. But as we pray, the Spirit of God helps us in our weakness and awakens deep longings and yearnings in our hearts for which we cannot find words (Rom 8:26). And God the Father, who knows and reads our hearts, reads there the mind and will of the Spirit, and He answers by sending the very events that are needed to work out the situation according to His purpose. There is a mighty, mysterious element about prayer, an element which, as God's people gather together and open their hearts and share their feelings with God, somehow creates an atmosphere for God to work in sudden, remarkable ways.

One night at a Young Life camp, at about eleven o'clock, the camp trumpeter was practicing out by the creek, all by himself. That, by the way, is where trumpeters should practice! When he finished, he put his trumpet away and came back to camp. But suddenly he was seized with an urge to play his trumpet in the middle of camp, and he felt that the urging was from God. So in obedience he took his trumpet out, put in the mute, and prepared to play. Then he thought, "What should I play?" The thought immediately came, "Play Taps!" So he played Taps with the muted trumpet. Then an inner voice seemed to suggest that he take the mute out and play it out louder. So he did. At 11:30 at night, in the middle of the camp, he played Taps out loud on his trumpet, put his instrument away, and went to bed.

The next day another young man described what had happened to him the night before. When he had first come to camp he had been belligerent and rebellious. He was not a Christian, and he didn't like what was going on. He decided he had had enough of it, and at about 11:30 at night he walked out of camp and headed toward the highway to hitchhike home. Suddenly he heard Taps being played on a trumpet. "I knew Taps was the song people played when somebody died," he said, "so I thought to myself, 'Who died?' And then the thought hit me, "Well, I know who died; it was Jesus. Jesus died, and He died for me.' " So he sat down by the road and received the Lord into his heart right on the spot. Surely someone's prayers for that boy were being answered that night!

Finally, notice how this chapter ends:

> But the word of God grew and multiplied. And Barnabas and Saul returned from Jerusalem when they had fulfilled their mission, bringing with them John, whose other name was Mark (Acts 12:24,25).

The Word of God grew and multiplied despite all the opposition. Two men whom God particularly wanted to instruct in how to handle tough situations—Barnabas and Saul—were keen observers of all that took place in Jerusalem at this time. Saul (Paul) would draw upon this experience many times later in his turbulent career—remembering how God could work to set people free, to open prison doors, to remove a tyrannical ruler—all in response to the believing prayer of His people. Let us also believe, and let us also pray.

God, I've Got a Problem
by Ben Ferguson·

Whatever man's problems, God's Word has insight for dealing with them!

God has provided Scriptural principles that can help us deal effectively with life's pressures. Insight into the truths of these inspiring principles are given in this helpful book by Ben Ferguson.

Pocket paperback $1.95

Ben Ferguson is a free lance writer for many Christian periodicals, whose practical Bible teaching makes him a popular conference and youth speaker. He is a graduate of California State University at San Jose and Dallas Theological Seminary in Dallas, Texas. Ben Ferguson is married and the father of four children.

Preparing for Adolescence
by Dr. James Dobson

One of America's leading Christian psychologists shares his expertise! The 10- to 14 year-old particularly needs his parents' guidance to form healthy attitudes and relationships. Dr. Dobson offers tools for parents to help their children prepare for the storms and turmoil of adolescence, including: **The Canyon of Inferiority** How to avoid feelings of inferiority…developing self-confidence ■ **Conformity in Adolescence** How to handle group pressure…dangers of drug abuse and alcoholism ■ **Explanation of Puberty** · Physical changes…sexual development …menstruation…masturbation…fear of abnormality ■ **The Meaning of Love** · The 10 most common misconceptions about love ■ **The Search for Identity** · Making sound decisions …overcoming discouragement …how to deal with feelings …handling independence.

A MUST BOOK FOR PARENTS AND KIDS ALIKE!

Paper $4.95

BOOK

WORKBOOK

PAK

Preparing for Adolescence Growthguide
A delightfully illustrated workbook of discussion-provoking ideas, plus self-tests and projects designed to encourage the teenager to think through important issues about himself and his beliefs.
Paper $4.95

Preparing for Adolescence cassettes
In the following six cassettes, he speaks directly to the pre-teenager in a friendly, casual manner. This portion of the series is available separately —already a best-selling album for individual use with pre-teens... in group discussions... in pastoral counseling.

Tape titles: "I Wish I Were Somebody Else" Self Esteem and How to Keep It · "I Think I've Fallen in Love" Understanding the Real Meaning of Love · "But Everybody's Doing It" Group Pressure and How to Handle It · "What Else Should I Know?" Introducing You to Yourself · "Something Crazy Is Happening to My Body" Understanding Physical and Sexual Development · "This Is How It Was with Me" Rap Session with Four Teenagers.
6 Tapes $34.98

Preparing for Adolescence Pak

Includes...
■ **Eight cassettes** In addition to the six tapes described above, Dr. Dobson has included two cassettes for parents and leaders. Pertinent guidelines to encourage adolescents through a meaningful program.

■ **Book**
■ **Growthguide** (See above)
Only $59.95

From the Heart of Joyce Landorf

Joyce presents sparkling highlights from her best-selling books. The following four cassettes are also available as singles, for $5.98 each.
4 Tapes $24.98

The Fragrance of Beauty ▪ Skillfully shows how to achieve an inner beauty that outglows all others.

His Stubborn Love ▪ Joyce shares the reality of a marriage on the rocks as well as the answers she and her husband found with God's help. These same answers may well improve your marriage.

Mourning Song ▪ With great sensitivity, Joyce talks about the tremendous trial of accepting one's own approaching death or that of a close family member. A truly inspirational and strengthening message.

The Richest Lady in Town ▪ Most women are passing up the wealth available through Christ as they seek artificial solutions to problems of personal fulfillment.

CASSETTES

CASSETTE

CASSETTE

CASSETTE

CASSETTE

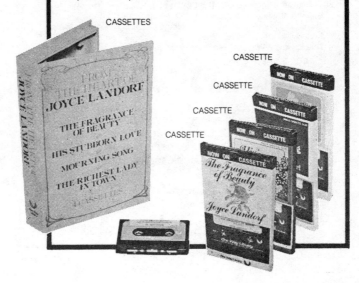

For These Fragile Times ■ At a time when human relationships are so easily shattered comes this cheerful message. Let Joyce tell you how life with those around you can become exciting and new! A refreshing breakthrough for developing lasting relationships. *Single Cassette $5.98*

Dinner Hour: Disaster or Delight ■ Don't let family feuds spoil another carefully planned and lovingly prepared dinner! Joyce offers hints for making mealtimes pleasant, sharing experiences for all family members. Bring your family together at the table tonight! *Single Cassette $5.98*

Tough and Tender ■ Joyce directs this message to men —as only a very sensitive and sensible wife and mother can. She's down to earth about the responsibilities of spiritual leadership in the home, and about "tuning in" to the daily considerations that can strengthen every marriage relationship. Every woman wants and can have a man that's tough and tender. *Single Cassette $5.98*

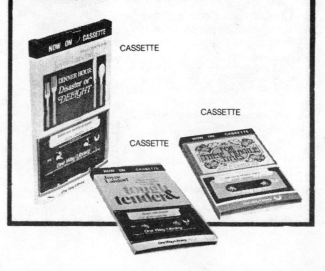

CASSETTE

CASSETTE

CASSETTE

Christian
Marriage

by Dr. Howard Hendricks

As most couples soon discover, marriage is only
as durable as its foundation, and as flexible as its
participants. In this fascinating guide to the
Christian perspective of marriage, Dr. Hendricks
demonstrates the clear relationship between faith
in God and marital depth and harmony.

Tape Titles:
What is Love? · Foundations of a Christian Marriage ·
Communication or Chaos · Purpose of Sex in Marriage · The
Role and Responsibility of the Husband · The Role and
Responsibility of the Wife

6 tapes available separately $34.98